Wise Publications
in association with Omnibus Press

▶▶ Preparation & Recording

▶▶ Doing the artwork of your CD

▶▶ Choosing a manufacturer

▶▶ Checklists

▶▶ Crucial sales strategies for your CD

▶▶ Choosing ISRC and EAN codes

▶▶ Legal questions relating to CD production

▶▶ Associations and institutions

▶▶ Founding your own label

▶▶ Technical details about CDs and DVDs

▶▶ Important information about the manufacture of vinyl records

▶▶ Appendix

Published by:
Wise Publications
8/9 Frith Street, London W1D 3JB, England.

Exclusive Distributors:
Music Sales Limited,
Distribution Centre, Newmarket Road,
Bury St. Edmunds, Suffolk IP33 3YB, England.
Music Sales Pty Limited,
120 Rothschild Avenue, Rosebery, NSW 2018, Australia.

Order No. AM976338
ISBN 0-7119-9805-1
This book © Copyright 2003 by Wise Publications.

Translated from the German by Kevin Colfer & Michael Widemann.

Cover design by Michael Bell Design.
Printed in the United Kingdom.

Your Guarantee of Quality
As publishers, we strive to produce every book to the
highest commercial standards.
The music has been freshly engraved and the book
has been carefully designed to minimise awkward page
turns and to make playing from it a real pleasure.
Particular care has been given to specifying acid-free,
neutral-sized paper made from pulps which have not
been elemental chlorine bleached. This pulp is from
farmed sustainable forests and was produced
with special regard for the environment.
Throughout, the printing and binding have
been planned to ensure a sturdy, attractive publication
which should give years of enjoyment.
If your copy fails to meet our high standards,
please inform us and we will gladly replace it.

www.musicsales.com

CHAPTER 1

►► Preparation and Recording

As you make the initial decisions about the production of your CD, 'Preparation and Recording' section covers each stage, from the idea in the rehearsal studio right up to the finished CD master.

Find out about

►► *Choosing the right songs*

►► *Choosing the right studio*

►► *How can a producer help?*

►► *Pre-mastering CDs on your own computer*

►► *CD-writers and the right CD-R*

►► *Checking the CD master*

►► *Mastering in a professional studio*

▶▶ *Choosing the right songs*

The A&R (artists and repertoire) manager at the record company receives your demo CD. It is their job to find and develop new talent. The main part of the A&R manager's work begins as soon as a new artist is found and the recording contract is signed. They develop an image for the artist and make marketing suggestions. The A&R manager is the first to be consulted when planning the release of a single or contributing a song to a CD sampler (also known as compilation CD). It is important for A&R managers to manage their time carefully as they only have a short time to go through the demo CDs and applications sent in by new artists. The same is true for concert and tour organisers as well as publishers.

Around 20 or 30 demo CDs arrive on the A&R manager's desk every day, so even if they allow themselves two hours to go through them all, they can only afford to spend between four and six minutes on each CD. This is something you have to bear in mind when you start planning a CD.

What is the point of your CD?
Choosing songs is the first step in planning a CD. You have to be clear about what you hope to achieve with it. There are two overall objectives.

1. Demo CDs (also called promotion CDs)
The aim of this kind of CD is to interest record companies, publishers or concert organisers. With promotion CDs it is enough to record your best songs for putting on to the CD later.

Making the most of studio time
CDs made for promotion purposes do not need more than three songs, a factor to bear in mind when considering which studio to use. Record only your best songs in the time you have available. Recording as many songs as possible is not suitable for what you are trying to do. If you concentrate on only a few songs and prepare them carefully, you will be guaranteed good results. You have time to polish up the arrangement of each song and to experiment with different sounds and microphones. The same applies to mixing. When you work on only one song per day, the results are likely to be far better than if you try to mix three or four songs in the same time.

Convincing the A&R manager with the right song
A&R managers will decide after the very first song whether a band has sufficient potential to sign to their company. If they are not convinced by the first song, they will listen to only one other track at most. If they do not see a hit in that either, the CD goes back in its case and you get a rejection letter in the mail.

You have only a few minutes to convince the A&R manager. Good songs are as important as good production.

This does not mean that a demo CD must have only a few songs. You can also send in a promotion CD with 15 or 20 songs. The important thing is that the CD starts with the best song and is well-produced. The first impression counts. Pick out the song that audiences seem to prefer and ask your fans which song is their favourite. You do not need an intro. Get right down to business with a cracker!

Show your full range
A&R managers who like your material will listen to all your songs. If you can sum up your whole range in three songs, then your chances of success are improved. That is why it is a good idea to choose different song styles from your repertoire for your demo CD. You can follow up your best at the beginning with a quieter song and then include a harder or more experimental number. This type of demo demonstrates variety and leaves people wanting more.

2. Recording CDs for sale
A different planning strategy is called for if you are aiming to sell CDs at gigs or in music shops. Your fans will hardly be satisfied with only three songs. Musical factors play a wider role in planning this kind of CD than with promotion CDs. Unlike A&R managers, normal listeners are likely to prefer an intro which gives them an idea of the CD's basic tone and which prepares them for what is to come. Wind or thunder noises create a gloomy mood, for example. Another possibility would be to use passages from films to loosen things up.

Another important point is that with this type of CD it does not matter where you put your best material. It could very well be track three, or it could come later to liven up the CD at the right time. The CD should still begin with a strong song, though, to convince the listeners right from the start.

▶▶ Choosing the right studio

Your choice of recording studio is one of the most important decisions when making a CD. The work you still have ahead of you is worth it when you have finished recording and are happy with the finished product. If you are not satisfied with the recording, it is not worth having the CD duplicated for distribution.

The cost of studios
Small recording studios for low-budget demo CDs cost around £150-300 per day. Within this price range you can expect a 24-track mixing console with either a multi-track tape recorder or a hard disk recording system.

These studios have enough different microphones and effects to give reasonable results. Good recordings are possible with good preparation and the right amount of time. You need to invest more, though, if you want more studio space, a larger mixing console and special microphones or effects. Large recording studios with the best equipment cost between £300 and £1,000 a day.

Gain from other musicians' experience

You can find the right recording studio by scanning the adverts in specialist magazines. It makes more sense, though, to take tips from musicians you know and those with experience. They are likely to know what you should look out for.

As soon as you have narrowed down your list to two or three, it is a good idea to visit each studio in person. That way you can get a good idea of the premises, the state of the equipment and the recording engineer you will be working with. Recording the vocals is particularly difficult. This kind of situation is critical and any friction between the musicians and the recording engineer will have a negative effect on the quality of your recordings. You will soon know from a face to face meeting whether you are on the same wavelength.

Does the studio specialise in one kind of music?

Ask the engineer to play you some sample recordings, so you get a good idea whether the studio specialises in one style of music or produces a broad variety. Both sorts of studio have advantages and disadvantages. A recording engineer who only ever does jazz recordings knows a lot about this type of music and knows what to emphasise. On the other hand, a recording engineer with little experience of jazz may be more prepared to experiment.

Take the chance to play the engineer some of your own rehearsal or demo recordings. That way they can get their first impression of your music and the instruments you use.

If all goes well, the recording engineer will like your music and, even at this stage, may make some production suggestions. If the engineer has absolutely no idea about your kind of music, look around for another studio.

▶▶ How can a producer help?

'The perfect producer makes a hit out of a song'. The producer is there to advise musicians in the rehearsal studio when they are preparing songs. A producer is also the link in the studio between the musician and the engineer. As a rule, engineers take on the producer's role with small recordings. During the recordings they give tips about individual songs and instrumentation.

It always makes more sense to include a producer in the studio work alongside an engineer, though it is not always easy to find the right person and cost is maybe an issue.

Working with the producer in the rehearsal studio
The first thing to understand is what the producer's job is and why they are important.

Producers must have a very wide-ranging musical taste and know a lot about various styles. They must have a good feeling for music and get to know your songs before you start recording. Good producers will listen to all your current songs and give an opinion about them. Even in the rehearsal studio they will help you to polish up your songs. They will give tips about the composition, the arrangements and make suggestions about instrumentation. In all these things the opinion of an outside professional is vital. You have played your own songs too often to be able to judge them objectively. Producers take on a big responsibility when they have a say in the structure of your songs and your band and, if you decide to work with a producer, you have to hand this responsibility to them.

Recording and mixing in the studio
The main job of the producer is to supervise in the studio and comment whenever someone plays out of tune, or the sound of the instrument does not fit in with the overall recording. At the mixdown stage the producer talks to the band and passes on a communal opinion to the engineer at the mixing console. That way you avoid individual musicians trying to push their instruments to the fore. Another job for the producer is keeping everybody happy and motivating them to do the best they can.

Finding the right producer
Producers used to be directly employed by the record companies themselves. Nowadays they work on a freelance basis, but have the same music industry contacts as they did before. It is easier for a producer to offer a recording to a record company than it is for a band. Producers know their contacts, and their contacts know them.

A&R managers are more likely to listen to material sent in by a producer they know than material sent in by an unknown band. There are two reasons for this. Firstly, producers know the A&R manager's taste and will only send them music they think they will like. Secondly, the A&R manager can talk more openly about the quality of the music with a producer they know personally.

If a producer is recommended by bands you know or by a record company, you have to do the same as you would when choosing a studio. Get the producer to show you some references. What kind of qualifications do they have?

Which bands have they worked with? What do they think of your music? Which contacts do they have in the music business? Then there is the most important question: how much do they cost?

Producers make their money by taking a percentage of the price of each CD. At professional level their cut is around 3-4% of the dealer price. Sometimes, however, they are also paid a fee. How producers are paid is different in each case and this is something which should be agreed before you start.

Many producers have their own production companies and will sign a contract with the musicians. The producer then finances the recordings and offers them to record companies.

You can find a producer among musicians you know

If you do not manage to find a professional producer, there is another alternative. Speak to a musician who makes and understands the same kind of music as you do, and who has already had some success.

They will have done enough recording and studio work to be able to fit into the role of producer. If they already have a recording contract, they will know who makes the important decisions in the industry. They will also do things cheaper than a well-known producer, and this does not necessarily mean they won't do as good a job.

▶▶ *Pre-mastering CDs on your own computer*

The pre-master is the CD-R from which the production master (called the glass master) is produced at the manufacturing company by 1:1 copying. You can find more detailed information about the way CDs are manufactured in chapter 10, starting on page 97.

To produce a glass master the manufacturer has to have a CD-R. If you send in a DAT (digital audio tape), the pre-master has to be made on site. The DAT has to be recorded onto a computer's hard disk and the starting points and pauses between the songs have to be reset. This is called P. Q. Editing. This involves further costs, and you lose certain artistic features such as the lengths of pauses between the songs.

To make sure you have all these details under control, you should either put the pre-master CD together in the studio or write the CD on your computer.

How can you edit the CD?

As regards software, there are a lot of possibilities. These range from shareware programmes which you can download free to professional tools costing a few thousand pounds. All mastering programmes have the same basic functions. You put your songs in a certain order on a play list and you determine how much of a pause there is between the songs. Certain tools also have functions which make it possible for you to adjust the volume levels of the individual tracks, especially important if you are making a compilation CD with different artists. It helps if you take one song as your guide which has an average volume level, then you make all the loud songs a bit quieter and the quiet ones louder. Making quiet songs louder does carry some risks, though. Listen to these songs again with particular care, checking for any crackles or interference which creep in when you turn up the volume.

CD-R, the cheapest way to make masters

From a professional point of view, CD-Rs are not the best way to generate masters. Each CD-R has errors which come about during recording. U-Matic tapes or DLT masters are the safer way of generating pre-masters. Both are digital recording systems with excellent storage qualities and high data security. After recording, the audio data on the tape will be compared 1:1 with the original material on the hard disk. That way the software keeps a record for checking purposes with all the data on the tape. These systems are very expensive, need a lot of maintenance and can only be found in professional mastering studios. So CD-Rs are the only economic option for having your own CDs replicated and this is what most people do. CD-Rs are sent to the manufacturer (also referred to as the replicator) in the production of around 95% of all CDs. U-Matic accounts for another 4% and DLT for only 1%.

If you choose a high-quality CD-R, there should not be any problems.

▶▶ CD-writers and the right CD-R

Nowadays just about every new computer is fitted with a CD-writer and it is not expensive to update old models. There is hardly any difference in the writing quality of the various models, though cheap CD-writers only have a short life-span. The choice of CD-R disk is a more common problem. Some types of writers are not compatible with the CD-Rs of certain manufacturers, this causes computer crashes and mistakes in the writing process. On the other hand, other writers work with CD-R disks without any problems. It is usually the CD-R disk and not the writer which causes problems.

The CD-R has become the most common way for storing data and doing backups, particularly on the computer market. CD-Rs have started to be mass-produced and competition between producers has led to pressure to keep prices down. This in turn has led to lower quality. Nowadays you can buy CD-Rs for around 50 pence.

Avoid cheap CD-Rs
Cheap 'no name' CD-Rs are not suitable for creating pre-master CDs. They are made of poor quality material and this, together with the extremely thin reflective coating, often leads to a high number of errors or loss of data. Stick to established brands and buy your CD-R in a music shop or in specialist shops. Investing up to ten pounds can save you a lot of trouble.

A slower writing speed means improved data security
When choosing the writing speed, you should take the time to write the CD at a speed of 1x. Whilst it is possible to write a lot quicker with modern writers, the laser only has a short time to write the data information. This increases the possibility of an error. Setting the rotation speed to 1x (maximum 2x) gives the laser enough time to write the data information precisely. This reduces the number of errors on the CD-R and increases its lifespan.

Writeable CDs are a very sensitive data storage medium which can easily be damaged by scratches or dirt. You should always store a CD-R in a CD case or something similar. When sending a CD in the post, take great care. Use padded envelopes and other similar protection. Cardboard sleeves are also ideal.

▶▶ Checking the CD master

A technical check is carried out at the manufacturer
When data is transferred from a CD-R by the manufacturer, they automatically carry out a technical check.

This means that the system checks how high the error rate of the original CD is. There are so-called black dots on every CD, places the laser cannot read. Thanks to error correction data, current CD players can even play CDs when up to 400 data blocks in a row are damaged.

During the manufacturing process other errors are added through wear and tear on the production master. This is taken into consideration when the glass master goes through quality control. Production of the glass master is stopped if a manufacturer receives a CD with too many errors.

The glass master system does not pick up every error during checking

Any dropouts on the CD-R (short spaces with silence or background noise) will not always be picked up by the glass master system as an error. That is why you must check the CD-R yourself before sending it to the manufacturer. Modern pre-mastering tools make it possible to check the CD-R after the writing process. The CD-writer reads the information on the CD and compares each bit with the data on the hard disk. If there is any error, write a new image file and generate a new CD from it.

Listen to the whole CD carefully

If the software does not find any errors during the checking process, then exactly the same data is on the CD-R as on the hard disk. Even though the CD-R has already been checked, give it a final check yourself. Take the time to listen to the whole CD-R with headphones.

Adjust the volume so you will not be distracted by noise around you. You must be able to hear the slightest error. Pay particular attention to the quiet parts and the changeover between songs. The last thing you should do is check the starting points of the individual songs. If the start-ID of a track is too far into the song, it will start too abruptly when the song is played using search facility.

Go through each song individually with the skip button and pay attention to the beginning of the songs. It is a good idea to put the starting point just before the song actually begins. It is more pleasant for the listener when there is a half second pause rather than the music starting straight away.

If the CD-R has passed all tests, it is ready to be sent to the manufacturer. Use a soft felt pen to name your CD-R on the disk itself as well as the inlay.

▶▶ Mastering in a professional studio

When recordings are being mixed in a studio each track is worked on separately. The recording engineer finds the right volume balance between the instruments and the vocal parts. They work on each individual instrument, bringing in different effects and using the available technology to alter the sound of each one. That way engineers can concentrate on individual characteristics of each instrument, emphasising or changing them.

Mastering enhances the overall recording

The individual tracks which make up a recording are not touched during the mastering process. The mastering studio receives the finished mix of recordings on a CD or a DAT as the input medium. There are no more basic changes to be made to the material at the mastering stage. Mastering is more about polishing up the music.

There are two parts to the mastering stage, the artistic side and the technical side.

Artistic aspects of mastering – final touches

It is essential that the engineer listens to the whole CD first. Engineers are specialists in mastering and have a very different ear for music. Mastering experts can notice things in each song that you miss. On the other hand, they could find some parts good which you don't like at all. You can discuss all of these things after listening to the complete CD together for the first time. The engineer will give you their impression and make suggestions as to how you can get more from the music. At this stage, you are looking to add the finishing touches. If the material still does not sound good after the final mixing in the studio, you cannot make any more major improvements during the mastering phase.

Condition of the material before the mastering stage

Any compressing of the input material for mastering should be kept to a minimum. Any necessary editing can be done more easily and exactly with uncompressed songs. Engineers will work on the tonal characteristics first to adjust the Stereophonic image and the Depth and try to make the music compact, while at the same time keeping the necessary transparency. They harmonise the sound of the individual tracks with each other to create an overall picture of the CD. Compressing the finished product comes at the end. Even if you can already do some of these things in the recording studio, you should leave them for the mastering stage. This is what mastering studios are for, unlike recording studios, which means that the equipment is better and the people who work there specialise in this kind of work.

The technical part of mastering – preparation for the manufacturer

When the sound of the music has been polished up, it is ready for the technical part of the mastering process. The audio material is made ready to be turned into the pre-master CD. Also, the starting points of the individual songs are set and given ISRC codes. You can find information about ISRC in chapter 6, beginning at page 73. Setting the pauses between the songs is also a part of this process.

There is no fixed pattern determining how long the pauses should be. Many CD manufacturers take two seconds as a rough guide, but the pauses can be longer or shorter. You can vary their length according to personal taste. The pause can be very short if a song at the end is faded out slowly, linking into the next one. On the other hand, if one song ends very abruptly and the following starts in the same way it is fine to leave three or four seconds between them.

Check the mastered material on a stereo system you are familiar with
The audio material is transferred on to a master after the editing phase. Depending on the studio, it is transferred on to a CD-R, U-Matic or DLT. You should keep a back-up copy on CD-R in any case, which you can take away and listen to on a stereo system you know well. That is the point when you can decide objectively if you are happy with your work.

In a good mastering studio the engineer will listen to the whole tape or CD again after it has been transferred on to a master. Only then is it ready to be sent to the manufacturer for replicating.

Mastering is a good idea, but expensive
Renting a mastering studio with an engineer costs between £50 and £100 an hour. You can expect to spend at least seven to ten hours working on a complete CD of around 50 minutes playing time. When making a decision about mastering, the financial aspect plays a large role.

Just as when you are choosing a studio, you should listen to a few of the mastering studio's samples and look around the premises first.

CHAPTER 2

▶▶Doing the artwork of your CD

You can improve your CD sales through booklet and inlay design and choice of packaging.
'Doing the artwork of your CD' tells you all you need to know about graphic design for your CD production.

Find out about

▶▶ *Different types of packaging*
▶▶ *Developing your design ideas on the computer*
▶▶ *Logos to work into the CD layout*
▶▶ *Specifications for films and digital art files*
▶▶ *Technical specifications for CD onbody label films*
▶▶ *Film output and checking*
▶▶ *PDF files*

▶▶ Different types of packaging

A few years ago one particular group brought out a single on CD in three different versions;

- ▶ as a 'special edition' in the usual plastic 'jewel case'
- ▶ as a Digipak in cardboard packaging with a plastic tray for the CD
  glued inside
- ▶ as a tin box

All three versions had a common design, all were sold for the same price and the same material was recorded on them. On the day of release the same number of each type was sent to the retailers, who were asked to display the three versions next to each other. Since the music and the design of the CDs were identical, customers based their decision solely on the packaging.

The sales result was surprising
Around 60% of customers went for the standard version in the jewel case, 30% for the Digipak version and only 10% for the tin box. When they were asked the reason for their choice, many customers said the same thing. The tin box was too impractical for most of them, as it did not fit in a standard CD rack and was awkward to handle. Their criticism of cardboard packaging was that it wears out a lot sooner than the jewel case and also does not readily fit in racks. The corners of the cardboard become worn and dog-eared and the teeth of the CD fastening clip in the plastic tray was easier to break off.

Production costs do not correspond to sales
Of all the types of packaging chosen, the jewel case is by far the best value for money. Digipak costs around twice as much to produce as the jewel case. The tin box is the most expensive to produce and will cost three or four times the jewel case.

So what have we learned from this?
Elaborate or expensive packaging does not automatically mean consumers like the product more. In fact, in this example the opposite was true.

Keep the results of our experiment in mind when you are planning

There are infinite options to package a CD in an elaborate and unique way. Things such as eye-catching packaging and poster-booklets with special embossing make your CD stand out from all the others but will result in excessively high production costs. Our example suggests the investment simply is not worth it. If you sell your CD at a gig, the music will be a fan's main reason for buying it. They will not buy it because it has 16 colour pages in the booklet or because it is in a Digipak.

There are cheap ways to design a CD packaged in a normal way which make it stand out.

We will now take a look at the most common ways to package a CD. You can also find the specifications of each type of packaging in this chapter, starting on page 31.

A paper sleeve is the cheapest way to package a CD

The sleeve is around 12cm x 12cm and is made out of normal white paper, as the name suggests. It has a circular window in it, so you can see the label. It is mostly used to package CDs which come with magazines and books and this type of packaging is ideal if the CD is a free gift, or if you are using it for advertising purposes, but is not the best if you are intending to sell your CD. Paper sleeves are not easy to close again properly once they have been opened. Another problem is that you cannot print anything on them, so you have no space to include a contact address and other information. That is also why this type of packaging is inappropriate for sending to contacts in the music industry.

Individually-printed cardboard sleeves

Cardboard sleeves are a good way to package demo-CDs. They are made in a similar way to a record sleeve. Cardboard sleeves are printed on both sides and have an opening slot for the CD. They are made of thick cardboard (around 250gsm) which make them relatively durable in comparison to paper sleeves. As they are not thick, cardboard sleeves save a lot of space (unlike the jewel case) and are practical for storage. Like paper sleeves, cardboard sleeves make the CD look like a freebie and are not suitable for CDs which are to be sold.

The classical jewel case

The most common type of CD packaging is the jewel case. It has a transparent lid with tabs to hold the booklet. The base is also transparent to make the inlay card visible. Trays, the plastic plates that hold the CD, are normally black, grey or transparent. It is possible, however, to get them in a range of various colours at an extra cost.

The booklet can be 2 to 32 pages long. The tabs of the jewel case cannot usually hold a booklet with more than 32 pages. Booklets with four or six pages are folded and those with eight pages or more are stapled together. Poster or concertina booklets are made by folding the paper several times, but are more expensive than stapled booklets even if they have the same number of pages. If the text of your booklet is what you are trying to draw attention to, a stapled booklet is your best option as it is easier to handle.

The inlay card fits into the back of the jewel case. In the standard layout it is printed on one side only. If the CD tray is transparent, it is sometimes printed on both sides. That gives you more space for designs which can be seen when the CD is taken out of the case.

Digipak

Digipak is more expensive and not as common. It consists of cardboard packaging with a tray glued inside. This type of packaging is known by different names, and each manufacturer has their own name for it. It was developed by an American firm, who first sold the product under the name Digipak. The Dutch firm Van de Steeg is licenced to make Digipak in Europe. The Berlin-based firm Topac calls it D-Pac, whereas a French manufacturer calls it Jade-Pac, and so on – the list is endless.

The product may have different names, but there is no difference in the quality or the way it looks. The only way you can identify the manufacturer is by looking at the trays glued inside. Normally they have the name of the firm stamped on them. This type of cardboard packaging can be made in different ways. Most combinations are possible, from four-page Digipaks with a tray and a cover lid to twelve-page Digipaks with two trays in cross fold. If you want to include a booklet with the CD, there are several ways to do it. One way is to have a die-cut slot in the cardboard on the inside next to the tray. This works for booklets with up to 24 pages. If you have more pages in your booklet, you either have to glue it down inside or put a separate pocket inside the packaging.

The booklet is inserted at the side, as with a cardboard sleeve. A pocket is not only cheaper than gluing the booklet down, but also more practical. It is difficult to turn the pages of a booklet glued inside the packaging, and the weight of the whole thing also makes it awkward.

Improving the appearance and lifespan of the Digipak
The finished cardboard packaging is coated with a shiny UV varnish which protects the cardboard against damage and makes it look nicer. You also have the choice of matt varnish which gives the packaging a silky feel and looks great. Use your imagination to add more features. The possibilities are endless. You could have a logo stamped on the cover or highlighted with foil. These little touches are beautiful but very costly.

Non-standard packaging
As well as the products described here, there are also plenty of other types of packaging, such as the tin box or special synthetic packaging. As these options are mostly impractical or too expensive, they have not caught on in the music business. The production costs involved are too great, especially when manufacturing on a small scale.

The idea behind shrinkwrapping
Wrapping the CD in cellophane is one of the last of the packaging stages. This means sealing the CD in a thin layer of PVC and is possible with jewel case CDs and cardboard packaging. Paper and cardboard sleeves can be sealed with shrinkwrap. Certain manufacturers produce CDs with a small thread/tab for peeling away the cellophane. If you have the choice, this is the better option. Having CDs wrapped makes sense if you sell most of them at gigs. This protects them in transit as well as on the sales counter and lets customers know they have a brand new CD.

If the CDs are sold in shops, having them wrapped makes little sense since many unwrap CDs to put security tags on them and to store the CD 'under the counter' to deter theft.

▶▶ Developing your design ideas on the computer

The CSD (Chartered Society of Designers) handbook contains a list of sample prices for various types of graphic design work. These tables show graphic designers how much they can charge for their design and development work. According to the handbook, a graphic designer can charge an average of £1000 for designing a booklet. That is, of course, only what the CSD suggests and is not binding. If you want to leave the design work to the professionals, you must expect to pay out at least £300. If your budget rules this option out, there is an alternative:

Do your CD artwork yourself
There is a choice of computer programmes offered by a whole range of firms with similar DTP layouts. One tool which is well-known and suitable for working on a PC is Corel Draw. If you are working on a Macintosh computer, you should take a look at Quark XPress. Manuals are available to show you how each programme works, so this chapter will be limited to showing you the important steps involved in designing your CD.

An eye-catching cover layout
Before you start work with the computer, you should have a basic idea of how the front cover is going to look. You may decide to use a photo or include a drawing, or maybe just text on a coloured background. There are no limits to how creative you can be in your design. It helps, though, to stick to some basic rules:

If the cover design allows, the name of the band or artist should go in the top third of the cover. If the CD is racked in a shop with only the top half showing, the name can then clearly be seen. This also applies when the CDs are lined up one after the other and customers flick through them like file cards.

If you want your CD to stand out, you need a cover layout that will attract the customer's interest. The right kind of cover design will also give the listener an idea of what kind of music to expect.

Avoid putting too much on to the cover. The more information on the cover, the less it will catch people's eye. Try to concentrate on what is essential and keep it simple. A good photo and the name of the band, or a striking drawing are the best way to attract attention. As soon as customers have the CD in their hands, they will turn it over – and that is where you can give them more information on the inlay card.

The steps involved

Scan pictures at the right resolution and save them

As soon as you have a basic idea of what you are going to do, you can start the more detailed work at the computer. The first thing to do is to scan the pictures, logos and text into the computer. When doing this, be sure to get the right resolution. The recommended resolution for pictures is 300 dpi (dots per inch), or 120 dpc (dots per centimetre). The abbreviation dpi/dpc tells you how fine the resolution is. Pictures on the Internet have a resolution of 72 dpi, which is not high enough for printing. At 72 dpi the con tours of your graphics will look like rows of dots and will not look clear to compensate for the enlargement.

When you set the resolution for what you are scanning, you must also bear in mind how large you want the finished picture to be. If the original image is only half as big as the finished picture is to be, you have to set the resolution at 600 dpi when scanning.

Don't rely on your computer screen

Computer screens are bright and can show colours a lot more intensively than most modern printing methods can. Print out your layouts from time to time. How your work looks on paper is the important thing. Unfortunately, even the printout from a good colour printer does not give a definite idea of how the finished product will look as the colours vary from printer to printer.

It is advisable to get a colour proof or Cromalin made. You can find more detailed information about this in this chapter.

Saving in the right format

You should save the pictures in file format TIFF or EPS which save pictures at exactly the same size as the original. JPEG and GIF format only have a small storage capacity and are not suitable for professional printing. They reduce the original files in much the same way as MP3-standard does with audio files.

The second most important element in your design is the type font

The right kind of font can give the CD its own character by emphasising the tone of the music. You can see how important the font is when you look at large companies such as Volkswagen or Daimler/Chrysler who had their own fonts designed that only they were allowed to use. This played a large role in helping them to set themselves apart from their competitors.

There are two basic types of font: serif fonts and sans-serif fonts. (The text of this book is set in a sans-serif font) The most common example of a serif font is 'Times New Roman', as used in newspapers or novels. 'Univers' is the best-known sans-serif font. Serif fonts are easier on the reader's eyes, whereas sans-serif fonts can look more modern. A serif font is advisable if there is a lot of text in your booklet and the print is very small. It does not matter so much if you only have a short piece of text, such as the name of the band or the titles on the inlay card. It is more important that the font fits in with the pictures and logos you have used.

Do not print the text too small

Text should not be smaller than five point. Text becomes readable from seven or eight point upwards, depending on the font. If the text is printed over a 4 colour picture rather than a single colour background, then you should go for a higher font size.

Always print out the layouts to test how easy they are to read in their original size. Font sizes often look different on the screen than when they are printed.

Bear in mind the manufacturer's specifications when setting out documents. They give information about the sizes and characteristics of the printed material. They will also let you know what you have to remember when producing the artwork for printing.

▶▶ Recommended logos for the CD

The Compact Disc was developed by the firms Philips and Sony and brought on to the market in 1982. Even today, these firms have the patent rights to all of the different types of CD available. That means that all manufacturers have to pay small royalties to Philips and Sony to make CDs.

These fees are already included in the manufacturer's price, so from a financial point of view you can forget about them. Philips and Sony do insist, however, on their compact disc logo being printed on every CD. Manufacturers are obliged to do this when they sign the licence contract, through few keep to the agreement in practice. This is something you should definitely make clear with your manufacturer. It is very possible for them to refuse to produce a CD if the compact disc logo is not on the artwork for the onbody printing.

That is all you need to think about as far as the CD's onbody print is concerned. It is wise, though, to include certain things which are standard. We have already talked about the compact disc logo which should be included. Other standard logos are the MCPS logo, the label code and small text usually written on the edge of the CD, which gives information about rules concerning copyright and performing rights.

Other things which normally go on the onbody are the name of the artist, the record company and the product catalogue number.

M C P S

The MCPS logo is not binding and can be put on to every CD. The content of every recording made in Great Britain is checked by MCPS, the Great Britain Mechanical-Copyright Protection Society. Your CD production is subject to the payment of royalties if songs and lyrics by MCPS members are included, even if the MCPS logo is not printed on the label. If it does not spoil the design of your label, you should include this logo. You then make it clear that MCPS copyright applies. More detailed information about MCPS registration can be found in chapter 8, starting on page 89.

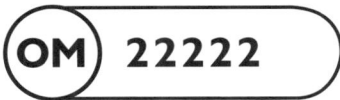

(OM) 22222

The label code is given to record companies. If your CD comes out on a particular record label, then its label code will be printed on your CD. It helps TV and radio stations when putting together official lists of the songs they play. These lists are used to work out the royalties that have to be paid to each label. See ISRC in chapter 6 page 74.

The small text around the edge of a CD often reads like this:
"ALL RIGHTS OF THE MANUFACTURER AND OF THE OWNER OF THE
RECORDED WORK RESERVED – UNAUTHORISED PUBLIC PERFORMANCE
AND COPYING OF THIS RECORD PROHIBITED"

ALL RIGHTS OF THE MANUFACTURER AND OF THE OWNER OF THE RECORDED WORK RESERVED • UNAUTHORIZED PUBLIC PERFORMANCE BROADCASTING AND COPYING OF THIS RECORD PROHIBITED

Copyright law is passed by the relevant legislative authorities. In Europe,
copyright is non-transferable, unlike in the USA. If you have an idea for a song for
example, you are always the originator. That even applies if you have not put the
above text on your CD.

It is different with performing rights, however. You have the option of
transferring performing rights to another person or company. From the moment
you sign a recording contract with a particular label, you transfer the performing
rights of your recordings to that company.

If the small text around the edge is not on your CD, then the person buying it
may get the impression that they have also bought the performing rights, too.
That would give them the right to use your recordings for their own commercial
purposes. In practice, this is the case with sample-CDs which include drum-loops
or keyboard sounds which the buyer can use however they like once they have
bought the CD. To avoid these misunderstandings, you should get this text
printed on the onbody label.

A | D | D

Another logo which is often used gives information about the individual steps
involved in the recording and production process. The logo has three letters. The
A stands for analogue, the D for digital. The first letter refers to the recording.
It will be an A if you record in an analogue studio. The second letter refers to the
mixdown stage. If your recordings are mixed in a digital studio, this letter will be
a D. The third letter gives information about mastering.

Besides these logos, the band or artist name should, of course, appear as well. It is a matter of personal taste whether you also have a list of the individual songs printed on the CD. That does not make a lot of sense, though, as the CD is invisible when it is being played, and there is very limited space on the CD itself.

Information on the inlay card
There is space on the inlay card for information about the songs. If you want to send the CD out to radio stations, DJs and venues as a promotion CD, you should also include the playing time of each song.

This makes it easier for DJs when they are planning their shows. You should also ensure a contact address is printed on the inlay card. A web site and email address should be enough. The only thing which is important is that concert organisers and record companies can contact you if they are interested. If you put an EAN bar code on the CD then you have to make it part of the design of the inlay card. You can find more detailed information about EANs in chapter 6, starting on page 75.

▶▶ *Specifications for films and digital art files*

All dates have been agreed with the manufacturer, and the manufacturer will be getting the films and the CD-R within the next few days. The manufacturers have said that the finished CDs are going to be delivered a day before the CD release concert. The venue and the sound system have been booked, the posters are already up and the flyers have been handed out. The CD release gig has been well planned. 200 fans are expected to turn up, who will each get a CD included in the cost of their entry ticket. About a week before the concert the manufacturers phone: the film for the label print has not been done properly and they need a replacement. It will take two days to get hold of the graphic designer and run the film again, another day to get the film delivered to the manufacturer, who say it is no longer possible for them to keep to the delivery deadline because of the problem with the film. The presentation has to be done without the CD.

This scenario is something every manufacturer is bound to have experienced, and you should prepare your materials correctly to avoid it happening to you.

When producing a CD, the most common errors are faulty or incomplete printing documents

In the next section you will find general specifications which apply to all printed documents to do with CDs. Although we go into great detail about every aspect, you should get your manufacturer to send their own specifications as there are differences between different manufacturers concerning printing areas and procedures.

In the specifications you will come across various technical terms, something which starts right at the beginning with the printing process.

Offset printing

Offset printing is a lithographic process in which a photo-sensitive metal plate prints the ink out thinly over the paper or cardboard. In special cases this process can be used to print CD labels, too. This kind of printing can be done in four-colour mode with the so-called standard process colours, in black/white or in special colours. The most usual of these is the four-colour mode. Colour printing works very much in the same way as a TV or computer screen (where primary colours red, yellow and blue are mixed to produce millions of different hues). In colour offset printing there are four standard process colours which are CMYK - Cyan, Magenta, Yellow and Key. Cyan is a shade of light blue, Magenta is pink, Y for yellow and K is for Key, which is black.

You only have an indirect influence on the process of breaking your picture down into these four primary colours. Make sure all your pictures are saved in the graphics software in CMYK mode (it is wrong to save them in RGB format). The separation of the colours into the four printing colours only happens in the reproduction studio during the film output.

Silk-Screen printing

In most cases the CD onbody label will be printed using in the screen printing process. It involves running the ink over the CD through a sieve (also called screen). Watch out for two things during the preparation of the label print films:

1. The choice of colours

Unlike offset printing, screen printing is not a process which involves colour mixing, but instead uses a spot colour process. With offset printing, it is possible to produce a rich shade of red by mixing Magenta and Yellow. This is not possible with screen printing. If, in the screen printing process, you print something in Yellow and then print over it in Magenta, the result is a slightly darker shade of Magenta. For this reason screen printing is done in special colours. There are two main producers for this ink along with a corresponding book of samples of each colour, HKS / RAL and PANTONE. The HKS book contains 46 different colours and PANTONE and RAL more than 1,000.

As a rule, manufacturers use the PANTONE Matching System (PMS). If you only have the HKS / RAL book available, you can also describe the colours you need using HKS / RAL numbers. The printer at the factory can then find out the equivalent shade in the PANTONE book.

2. Image resolution

With screen printing it is not possible to have such fine resolution as with offset printing. When a black-and-white picture is printed, the different shades of grey (the so-called grey scales) are made by an uneven distribution of individual black dots. You can see dots in the pictures in newspapers or when you stand right up close to a large poster. Offset pictures are printed using a 60 screen, which means that a centimetre is divided up into 60 dots. With screen printing, you can only have a 40 point screen and the structure of the screen determines the distribution of the dots. If film with a finer resolution is delivered, screen printing will not produce clear results. The continuous tones will look blurred and unclear. If you want to print a black-and-white background picture on a label printed in two colours, make sure the background picture has contrasty tones. Too many grey tones disappear with screen printing and are difficult to make out.

The importance of trim marks and the bleed

Booklets, inlay cards and cardboard packaging are printed on large sheets and later cut to size by use of trim marks (a process known as trimming). It is very risky to print in the same size as the final format. If a sheet were to slip half a millimetre out of place when the booklets are being cut, it would cause a 'flash' where a thin white stripe can be seen. To avoid this, add a 2mm trim or bleed to your pictures and backgrounds. (Bleed refers to layout, type or pictures that extend beyond the trimmed edge on a page.)

An example

The markings on the corners show the cover of this book in final, trimmed format. You can clearly see the trim marks and the crosshair mark (also referred to as registration mark).

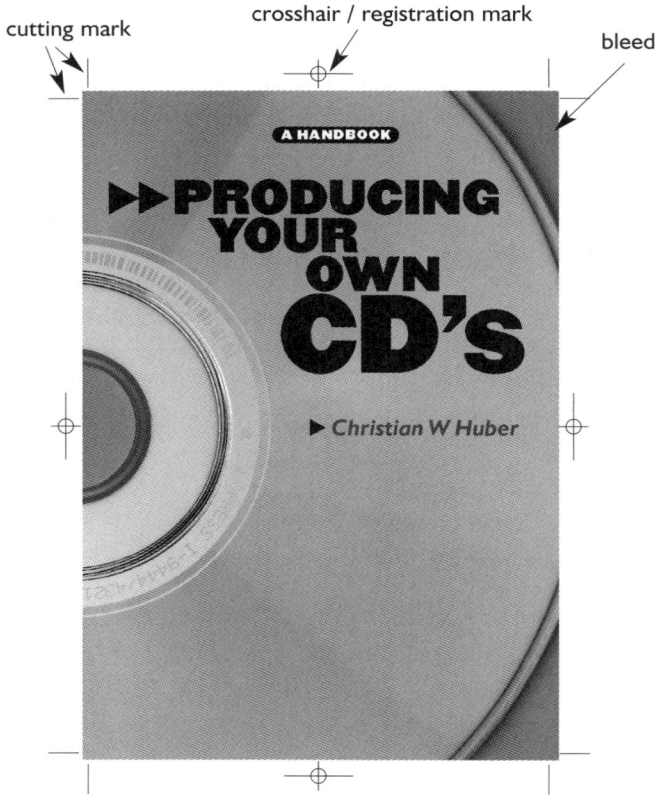

You must not set trim marks when the image is to be printed on to the CD onbody. Printing the label is always the last step in the process of manufacturing a CD. You must make sure the film and the available print area of the disc are exactly the same in order to stop the ink running over the edge of the CD during printing.

Specifications

In the next part you will find general printing specifications which apply to CDs. Although in great detail, you should still ask your manufacturer to send you a copy of their specifications and compare the two.

Booklet with 4 pages

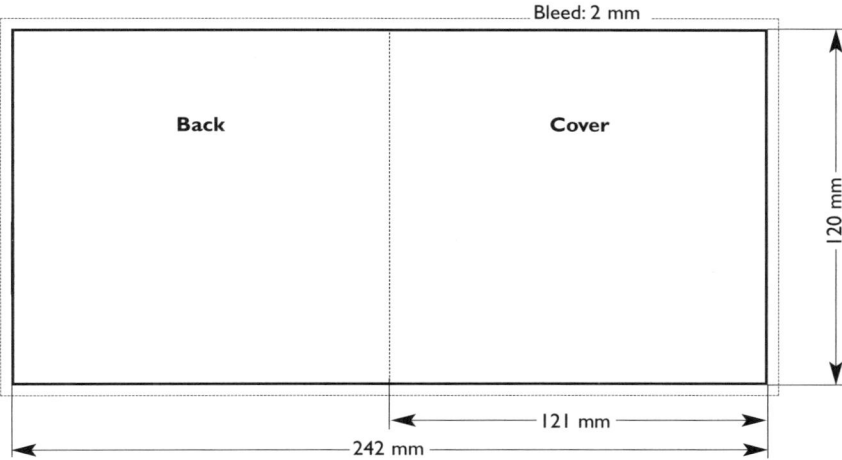

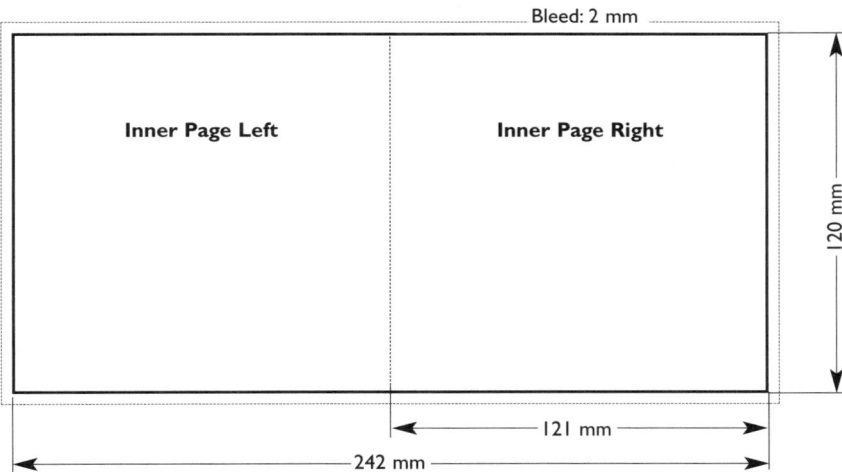

```
............................ Bleed: 2 mm ............................

┌─────────────────────────────────────────────┐   ▲
│                      ¦                        │   │
│       Back           ¦          Cover         │  120 mm
│                      ¦                        │   │
└─────────────────────────────────────────────┘   ▼
            ◄──────── 121 mm ────────►
◄──────────────── 242 mm ────────────────►
```

```
............................ Bleed: 2 mm ............................

┌─────────────────────────────────────────────┐   ▲
│                      ¦                        │   │
│   Inner Page Left    ¦    Inner Page Right    │  120 mm
│                      ¦                        │   │
└─────────────────────────────────────────────┘   ▼
            ◄──────── 121 mm ────────►
◄──────────────── 242 mm ────────────────►
```

Technical specifications for the booklet films

Condition of films

Offset films (positive film right reading emulsion down) with colour identification as well as the necessary marking (crosshair marks, cutting marks and trim) on each film. A colour proof (e.g. Cromalin) is highly recommended. Small discrepancies between the proofs and the final result are possible.

Format

242mm (121mm per side) x 120mm + 2mm trim

Screen count

150 lines/inch (60 lines/cm)

Assembling the pages

The pages must be assembled according to the technical drawing (2 pages together). Otherwise you could be charged for having the booklet film assembled. Follow the assembly imposition instructions on the following page if your booklet has more than six pages.

Assembly imposition for booklet pages

4 Pages

4	1
2	3

8 Pages

8	1
2	7
6	3
4	5

6 Pages

5	6	1
2	3	4

12 Pages

12	1
2	11
10	3
4	9
8	5
6	7

16 Pages

16	1
2	15
14	3
4	13
12	5
6	11
10	7
8	9

20 Pages

20	1
2	19
18	3
4	17
16	5
6	15
14	7
8	13
12	9
10	11

Inlay card for jewel cases

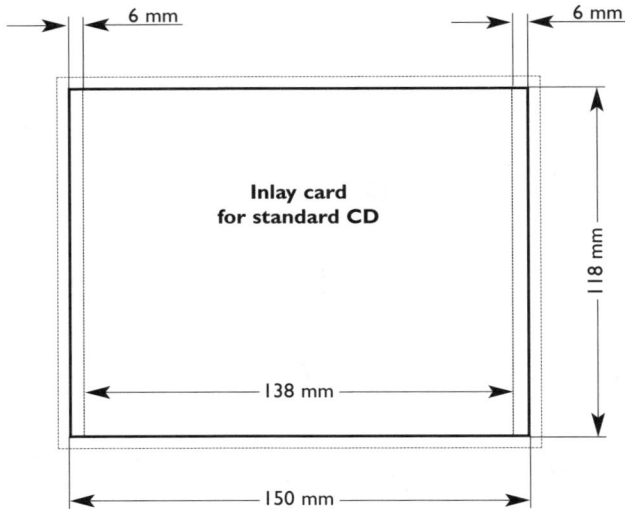

Technical specifications for inlay card films

Condition of films
Offset films (Positive right reading emulsion down) with colour identification as well as the necessary marking (crosshair marks, cutting marks and trim) on each film. A colour proof (e.g. Cromalin) is highly recommended. Small discrepancies between the proofs and the final result are possible.

Format
150mm (including 2 flaps of 6mm each) x 118mm + 2mm trim on each side.

Screen count
150 lines/inch (60 lines/cm)

Maxi inlay card / CD single card

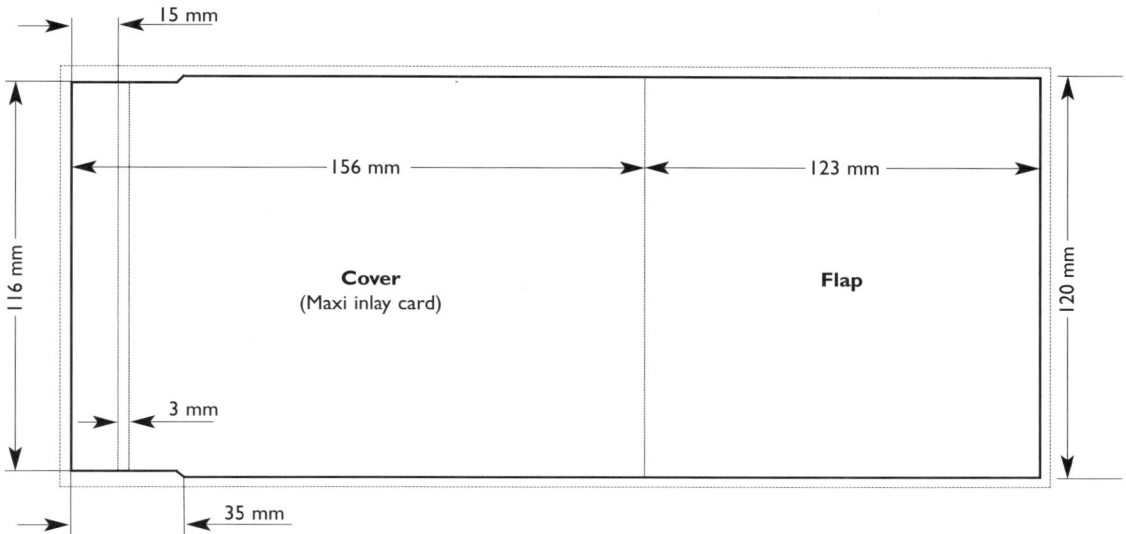

Technical specifications for maxi inlay card films

Condition of films
Offset (Positive right reading emulsion down) films with colour identification as well as the necessary marking (crosshair marks, cutting marks and trim) on each film. A colour proof (e.g. Cromalin) is highly recommended. Small discrepancies between the proofs and the final result are possible.

Format
279mm (including a 3mm flap) x 120mm + 2mm trim on each side.

Screen count
150 lines/inch (60 lines/cm)

Cardboard sleeve

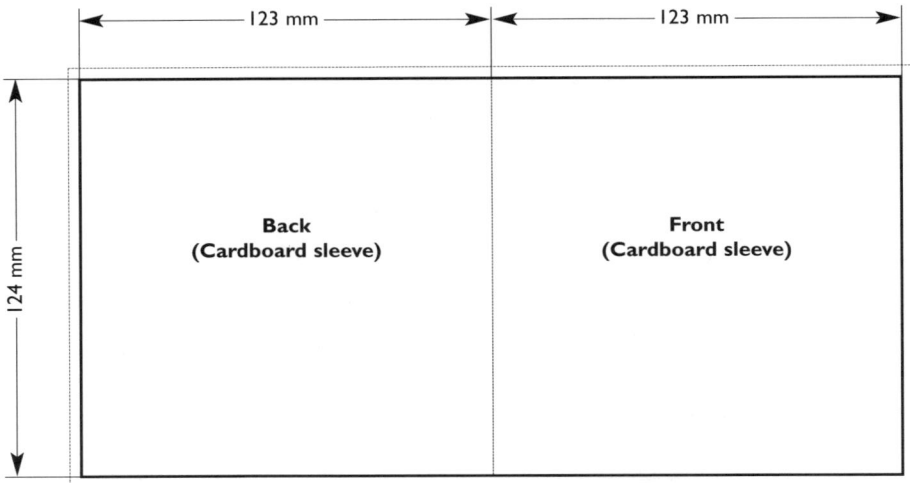

Technical specifications for the cardboard sleeve films

Condition of films
Offset (Positive right reading emulsion down) films with colour identification as well as the necessary marking (crosshair marks, cutting marks and trim) on each film. A colour proof (e.g. Cromalin) is highly recommended. Small discrepancies between the proofs and the final result are possible.

Format
123mm x 124mm (actual size of the sleeve) + 2mm trim on each side. Both the front and the back have to be assembled as in the diagram above. Otherwise you will have to pay to have the sleeve assembled.

Screen count
150 lines/inch (60 lines/cm)

Silk-screen Printing, Label 12cm

120 mm - size of CD
117 mm - printing area
20 mm
35 mm
46 mm

Silk-screen Printing, Label 8cm

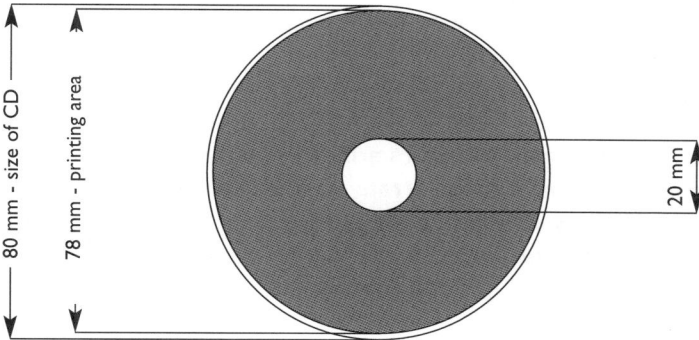

80 mm - size of CD
78 mm - printing area
20 mm

Technical specifications for CD onbody label films

Condition of films
Films have to be positive, right reading with emulsion side up (With offset films the emulsion side has to be down). All films must contain the necessary marking (colour identification as well as crosshair and centring marks)

Printing format: 12cm CD
▶ 117mm - 20mm / 117mm - 35mm / 117mm - 46mm

Printing format: 8cm CD
▶ 76mm - 20mm / 76mm - 35mm

▶ A white background surface is recommended if a centre circle diameter of 20mm is chosen, since the surface between 35mm and 20mm is transparent, not metal-coated. Make sure you deliver a corresponding film for the full surface. Remember if you use white, this is a separate printing and should be included in the number of colours used.

▶ The technical circles of the outside and inside diameters must not appear on the films at all.

▶ There must not be any trims.

▶ A circular space as big as the desired inner diameter should be left on the films.

Printing ink
Only Pantone colours are used. Pantone colours are direct colours , i.e. they can not be mixed, which means they have to be arranged in angles and must not be printed over one another. That is why there should be a corresponding space set aside for motifs or text on the rest of the films, especially if they are dark-coloured.

A standard label print includes one or two Pantone colours, but it is possible to print them with up to five colours from the entire Pantone book.

Screen count
100 lines/inch (40 lines/cm)

Cardboard packaging with tray glued inside

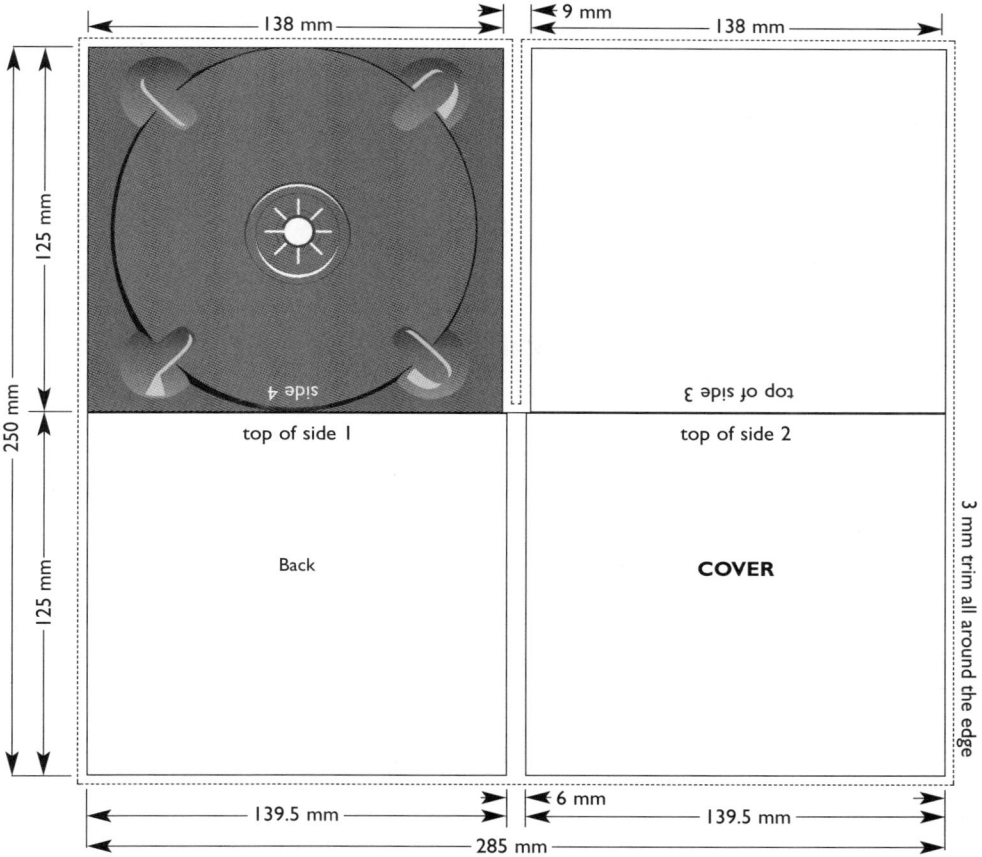

Technical specifications for the delivered films

Condition of films

Offset films with colour identification as well as the necessary marking (crosshair marks, cutting marks and trim) on each film. A colour proof (e.g. Cromalin) is highly recommended. Small discrepancies between the proofs and the final result are possible.

Format
Open: 285mm x 250mm + 3mm trim
Final format (when closed): 139mm x 6mm x 125mm

Screen count
150 lines/inch (60 lines/cm)

Assembling the pages
The pages must be assembled according to the technical drawing. Otherwise you will be charged for having the booklet assembled.

▶▶ Transferring the computer data on to film (film output)

Manufacturers often add the following to their literature:
"Prices apply on receipt of a transfer-ready CD-R and all films needed for printing."

You need to get films of your computer data made. Typesetting and reproduction studios can do this for you. You can find addresses of such studios in your local phone book. The printing plates and screens are copies from the films made by the printer.

Agree with the reproduction studio which programmes should be used
Before you get your graphic files ready to be transferred on to film at a reproduction studio, you have to discuss the formats. Find out whether they work with a Macintosh or PC.

It is also important that your software is compatible with the programmes of the studio. As a rule, lithographers work with Quark XPress or InDesign and sometimes with Corel Draw. Even if you have designed your layout with a programme which is not used in the reproduction studio, you have the option to save your finished layouts in TIFF-format. Make sure you have the right resolution, at least 300 to 500 dpi. TIFF files can be opened on any computer and can therefore be transferred on to film in any reproduction studio, though it is still important to discuss all the details with your reproduction studio.

Film output and checking

The only thing about the films which manufacturers check is that the technical specifications are right – whether all the fonts have been correctly interpreted or whether the pages of the booklet have been assembled in the right order.

There should be four films for each colour page, which are marked Cyan, Magenta, Yellow, Black or with the corresponding initials CMYK. Only one film is necessary for a black/white page. The films should have all the necessary markings (crosshair, cutting and trim marks). The crosshair marks make it possible to line up the four colours exactly when the films are put together on top of each other (see the example of the book cover on page 30). The trim marks are used after printing to ensure the booklets are cut correctly.

Mark the order of the booklet pages on the films outside the trimmed page area with a marker pen as shown in the specifications on page 33.

The onbody label film is a common source of errors

When checking the film, pay special attention to the label films, comparing it with the manufacturer's specifications. There should be a space left for the hole in the middle of the CD. Similarly, your graphics should not spread out further than the image area on the outer edge of the CD. Technical drawings showing the inner and outer diameters of the CD should also not be visible on the film.

How can you tell the difference between a silk screen and an offset film?

Reproduction studio staff often fail to register that a CD onbody label to be printed is a silk screen printing job; they are used to do all films for offset printing. The films can only be told apart by the side the emulsion is on. With a silk screen film the layer of emulsion is on the top and with offset film it is on the bottom – something which is difficult to see with the naked eye.

Place the film in front of you so that the text and pictures are reading the correct way round. Then scratch a crosshair mark outside the area to be printed. If the image comes off, then the emulsion is on the top and you have a silk screen film. If no image comes off, it must be an offset film. Though there seems to be little difference between offset and silk screen film, the manufacturers cannot work with a film that has not been correctly run. This will lead to unnecessary extra costs and may hold up production.

The cost of film

For booklet films you will be charged for A4 films. A4 exposure costs £4.50-6.50. Five films are required for a standard booklet, four for the coloured cover and one for the black & white interior. Inlay card and label film are A5 and come to around £3-5 on average. You need four films for the coloured inlay card plus another two for the label.

Expect to pay out around £40-60 for film output for a standard CD.

It is advisable to include a laser print with the films which the printers can then use to check the order of the booklet pages, and approximate colours.

▶▶ PDF files

It is also possible to supply the manufacturer with digital files of your artwork as PDF format files on CD. This is a way of avoiding the cost and complication of supplying printing film, but can be less accurate for colour and can involve extra charges from your manufacturer. PDF files are made by using Adobe Acrobat Distiller software. A colour laser print should always be supplied with a PDF file of artwork for identification and guide to image layout.

CHAPTER 3

▶▶Choosing a manufacturer

Your finances play an important role in your decisions. 'Choosing a manufacturer' contains examples of cost calculations plus tips about handing over the job and how it should be done.

Find out about the following:

▶▶ *How do you find the right manufacturer?*

▶▶ *What to look out for*

▶▶ *The full costs of producing a CD*

▶▶ *Delivery of the CD*

▶▶ *What if anything goes wrong?*

▶▶ *How do you find the right manufacturer?*

You can find advertisements for CD manufacturers and brokers in *New Musical Express* in other magazines and through the internet. Brokers only provide a service and do not have any manufacturing facilities of their own but may work for one or more manufacturers.

Take advantage of the services brokers have to offer
Since brokers assure manufacturers of a large volume of work, they get advantageous terms, which they can pass on to their customers. It is often cheaper to arrange a job through a broker than dealing directly with a manufacturer. In addition, brokers often offer services not normally offered by manufacturers. These include things such as consultation when registering with MCPS, putting together the graphics for the CD and film/PDF output, as well as mastering and pre-mastering the audio material.

They can also offer additional services, which can be very useful. These range from advice and ideas about going online with your own homepage to finding contacts within the music industry.

Manufacturers, however, limit themselves purely to replicating audio and data carriers. Some offer other services, but these tend to be the exception.

The advertisements you will see in the music and specialist press are almost always for brokers. Manufacturers prefer to work with agents, as they do all the customer advice work and checking of input media, limiting their advertising to trade magazines and exhibitions.

Working with a broker is to your advantage. Unlike the manufacturers, they specialise in small-scale productions, can take more time over each job and can offer more personal advice.

Shop around before you start
When getting estimates, price is not the only thing you should look at. The cheapest offer is not automatically the best value for money. If you have limited your choice to two or three brokers, it is a good idea to speak to them all by phone. This gives you the chance to form your own impression of each firm.

If communication is already good between you at this initial stage, it will continue the rest of the time you are working together on the CD. This would make a big difference if anything were to go wrong.

You should be wary if you always only get the answering machine when you ring a particular broker, or it takes them a week to deal with your enquiry. It is best to give these firms a wide berth.

Make personal contact

If you find a broker in your local area, you can get to know your contact person there face-to-face, discuss deadlines and production details and get them to show you samples of their work.

You can also hand your material over to them personally. Your contact can check the films there and then and suggest solutions if there are any mistakes. You can also get them to give you written confirmation that they have accepted the job.

Check offers carefully

When you are checking manufacturers' prices, you must make sure their offers are identical. Two examples from advertisements in music magazines show why this is important.

Example 1

1000 CDs for £300 (CDs in bulk on spindle, excluding glass master costs, postage and VAT).

Example 2

1000 CDs for £800 (ex films, CD master and delivery. Including glass master, 4-page booklet (4/1), inlay card (4/0), jewel case and tray, packaging and VAT).

It is impossible to say which offers the best value, as there is such a big difference in what is included in each case.

You should be very cautious about example 1, though, as it does not say much. It is impossible to produce a CD without a glass master, so why is there no glass master price included? CDs delivered on spindles do not include a booklet, inlay card or jewel case. How much will all these items add up to? How much are the postage costs? What's more, prices given in magazine advertisements must always include VAT, and that is missing here.

The second example is far clearer. You give them the films for printing and a CD master and you get a CD with all the standard feature, ex-works, for an all-inclusive price of £800.

It only makes sense to compare prices which apply to the same production process and features.

▶▶ What to look out for

The latest you should phone a manufacturer is when you have decided to give them the job. Let them know that you are giving the work to them and that the material will soon be on its way.

When you do that you can also discuss all the questions in advance which become important during production:

Which address do you have to send the material to and to whom?
With large firms in particular it is important to have a contact who looks after the job at every stage and can be contacted if you have any questions. If you want to talk about deadlines or stay informed about how things are coming along, this person knows everything about your particular job.

What is the order form?
Some firms enclose an order form with their offer, which you can send back to the manufacturer together with the documents. Order forms help, but are not strictly necessary. It is enough if you enclose a letter with the order, containing the production details. The most important points are your address, the quantity required, how you would like them done and when you would like them to be done by. The letter should be addressed to your contact.

Will the manufacturer contact you when they have received the material?
There are several advantages to this. Firstly, you know for sure that the manufacturers have received the documents. Secondly, your contact person has the documents in front of them and can discuss all the details with you. If some of the documents are missing, or if there is anything wrong with them, you have the chance to get replacements quickly.

What are the terms of payment?
Most firms insist on a deposit. Discuss the amount (50% of the whole cost of the job is normal), and by which date it has to be paid. This is especially important when the delivery deadline is tight. The manufacturer will not deliver your order if they have not received your deposit. In addition, you should find out whether the rest is to be paid by credit transfer, cheque or on delivery. If the latter, you should have enough cash on you when the delivery is made.

How will the CDs be delivered?
Small orders of up to 300 CDs are sometimes delivered by courier firms or by post. You should be there to receive the goods yourself, or get someone else to take them for you. Ask the manufacturer to let you know when they are going to deliver.

CD-AUDIO / CD-ROM ORDER

ORDERER / ADDRESS OF INVOICE:

Company:...

Name:..

Street:...

Postal Code / City:...

Telephone:..

Facsimile:..

ADDRESS TO DELIVER: (when different)

Company:...

Name:..

Street:...

Postal Code / City:...

Telephone:..

Facsimile:..

SUPPLIED MEDIA:

Artist:.. Title:...

❑ DAT   ❑ CD-R   ❑ U-Matic

❑ Other:............................ ❑ CD Label   ❑ Printing Matters / Films

COMPACT DISC:

❑ Standard CD (max. 74 min.)

❑ Maxi CD (max. 21 min.)

❑ Multiple CD

❑ CD-Rom

❑ CD-Extra (Audio + ROM)

EDITION:

⇨ ....

⇨ ....

⇨ ....

⇨ ....

⇨ ....

LABELPRINT:

❑ 1-2 Colours (Silk-Screen Print)

❑ 3 Colours (Silk-Screen Print)

❑ white baselayer (20mm / 117mm)

❑ 4 Colours (offset)

PACKAGE:

❑ Standard Jewelcase with black Tray

❑ Standard Jewelcase with white Tray

❑ Maxi-Slimbox

❑ Multibox (for 2-4 CDs)

❑ Brillantbox (for 2 CDs)

❑ Cardboardbox CD-Pac / Metalbox

❑ Cardboard Sleeve (1-4 colours)

❑ Supply without packaging on spindle

❑ Others:...

PRINTING MATTERS:

❑ Booklet (outside 4 colours / inside b/w) - Page #:.......

❑ Booklet (outside & inside 4 colours) - Page #:.............

❑ Inlaycard (single side 4 colours)

❑ Inlaycard (outside & inside 4 colours)

❑ Maxicard (single side 4 colours)

❑ Maxicard (outside & inside 4 colours)

❑ Supply without printed matter

❑ Others:...

Herewith I charge the company .... to produce the products listed above.

....
City, Date

....
Signature

Make sure you're easy to contact

If you fail to receive the shipment personally and examine the package for possible damage, you could lose your right to complain. In the case of a dispute, drivers may say there was nothing wrong with the parcel when they delivered it. Otherwise you accept all responsibility for the delivery.

Your manufacturer can arrange for the courier firm to ring you the day before the goods are due to arrive, making it possible for you to arrange a delivery time.

When you have agreed on all these points, your CDs are ready to be made. Pack your documents as securely as possible when sending it to the manufacturer. You should also consider having it sent by courier or recorded delivery. That way your material is insured and you will be compensated if it gets lost.

▶▶ The full costs of producing a CD

If you take all costs into account when planning your CD, there should be no financial problems on the way.

The following calculations take into account all the costs incurred, starting with generating the audio CD master. The examples do not include the studio and mastering costs, since the prices are so different. It is possible to rent a demo or project studio for £150-300 per day. The bigger and more modern the studio is, the higher the costs are. If you have to manage on a small budget, you should choose a cheap studio, but plan more studio time.

The costs for MCPS in general cannot be included, either. The rate depends on the material on the CD, the retail price and the playing time. If your CD only contains songs of an artist who is not a member of MCPS, there will not be any MCPS royalties.

If, on the other hand, songs of famous artist(s) have been covered, you will have to pay royalties to MCPS. In chapter 6, starting on page 73, you will learn how you can calculate the MCPS costs for your CD and how you can register your recordings.

Watch out for VAT

When working out costs, check whether prices include VAT (Value Added Tax) or not (17.5 % as correct January 2003).

Prices in advertisements or on the Internet should always be inclusive prices, in which VAT has already been calculated. In price lists you get directly from the manufacturer or from a broker, the prices are exclusive of VAT and you must add 17.5% VAT. You should always use the inclusive price when calculating costs, as this is the price you will end up paying.

NB: If you see the words "The net amount is payable on or before ..." on some invoices next to the final total, it does not mean you only have to pay the net amount excluding VAT. Some firms give you a 2-3% discount if you pay within a few days of receiving the invoice. This is called a cash discount. If a firm does not give a cash discount, the phrase given above makes this clear (net amount). You still have to pay the whole amount in full.

What follows are sample calculations to give you some idea of what to look out for when planning your CD production.

Calculation No.1:
Artwork for a standard CD, film output, manufacture of 1,000 CDs and promotion costs.

Artwork:

10 hours @ £30 ....£300.00

Material costs for printouts etc. £30.00

Film output:

Booklet: 4 A4 films for the outer pages,

plus one A4 film for the inner page @ £6 ....£30.00

Inlay card: 4 films and label print 2 A5 films @ £5 ....£30.00

CD replication (ex transfer-ready CD and all films):

Glass master £185.00

Manufacture of 1,000 CDs @ £0.30 ....£300.00

1,000 booklets and inlay cards @ £0.12 ....£120.00

1,000 jewel cases plus trays @ £0.10 ....£100.00

Promotion costs (postage to 50 music magazines):

Postage and packing @ £1.50 ....£75.00

Subtotal £1,170.00

17.5% VAT £204.75

Total cost **£1,374.75**

Calculation No.2:
CD in 6-page cardboard packaging with a glued-in tray, matt varnished and a 12-page colour booklet, artwork, film output, manufacture of 1,000 shrinkwrapped CDs and stickers.

Digipak artwork:

8 hours @ £30..£240.00

8 hours for the booklet @ £30 ....£240.00

Material costs for printouts etc.................................£100.00

Film output:

4 A2 films @ £20..£80.00

Booklet: 24 A4 films for A4 booklet @ £6 ....£144.00

Label print: 2 A5 films @ £5 ....£10.00

CD replication (ex transfer-ready CD and all films):

Glass master..£185.00

Manufacture of 1,000 CDs @ £0.30 ....£300.00

1,000 12-page booklets @ £0.27................................£270.00

Cardboard packaging with glued-in tray: 1,000 @ £0.50...........£500.00

Matt varnishing x 1,000 @ £0.10...............................£100.00

Shrinkwrapping x 1,000 @ £0.03 ....£30.00

Putting on stickers (by hand) x 1,000 @ £0.04 ....£40.00

Subtotal...£2,239.00

17.5% VAT £391.83

Total costs..**£2,630.83**

Calculation No.3:

Artwork for a Maxi CD, film output, manufacture of 500 CDs and postage costs to record companies.

Artwork for the Maxi CD:

4 hours @ £30 ....£120.00

Material costs for printouts etc. £20.00

Film output:

Maxi inlay card: 4 A4 films for the A4 outer pages @ £6 ....£24.00

Label print: 2 A5 films @ £5 ....£10.00

Maxi CD replication (ex transfer-ready CD and all films):

Glass master up to 21 minutes £110.00

Manufacture of 500 CDs @ £0.40 ....£200.00

500 Maxi inlay cards @ £0.12 ....£60.00

500 Maxi slimboxes @ £0.10 ....£50.00

Postage costs to 10 record companies:

Material costs and postage @ £3 per company £30.00

Subtotal £624.00

17.5% VAT £109.20

Total costs **£733.20**

These calculations are based on an average price of several manufacturers and are only included to give you an idea of cost breakdowns. You should, of course, get quotations for your own production from several manufacturers and compare them.

▶▶ Delivery of the CD

Why is there a 10% over/under difference?

You will find the following clause in manufacturers' order confirmations as well as in their terms and conditions:

"For technical reasons the number of CDs delivered can be +/- 10% different to the number ordered. The actual number of CDs delivered will appear on the invoice."

If you order 1,000 CDs, you very rarely get exactly 1,000. It is normal to get a few more or a few less.

Replicating CDs is a process which is prone to problems and errors. The number of rejects is around 5-10%, which is included in the manufacturing cost. That is why they make a batch of 1,100 CDs whenever they get an order for 1,000. Each CD is tested after the replication and the label printing. The first thing to be checked is the digital audio material. The next thing to be checked is that the labels have been printed correctly. Defective CDs are discarded if they fail to pass either test. As it is difficult to say beforehand how many CDs will be discarded, you may order 1,000 CDs but only get 950. You may even get 1,050.

All CDs delivered have been checked

The checking process assures you that all the CDs you receive will be of perfect quality. This really is the case: statistics show that the number of defective CDs sent back to manufacturers is almost zero.

The manufacturers will only charge you for the exact number delivered. If you only receive 950 CDs, you only pay for 950. The same applies if you receive more than you ordered.

How long is the manufacturing process (also referred to as the turnaround time)?

It takes around five to seven working days to produce a standard CD. Then add on one or two working days delivery time, giving an average time scale of seven to nine working days. You should therefore plan around two weeks for production of a standard CD in a jewel case.

Special packaging takes longer to produce

Manufacturers do not normally make special packaging themselves. If a manufacturer buys Digipaks from another producer, it takes time to have them delivered. In addition, certain special types of packaging have to be assembled by hand, a crucial factor when manufacturing on a large scale. It is important to discuss delivery times with manufacturers in detail if your order includes non-standard CDs.

Place your order in good time

If you place your order early enough and discuss all delivery deadlines in advance, you can have your CDs finished in three or four working days. It all depends on how flexible your manufacturer is and how heavy a workload they have. Difficulties can arise in November and December. The run up to Christmas is the most important time of the year for music retailers, which means manufacturers often have very full schedules around this time.

Getting your CDs delivered without problems

Courier firms can handle small orders and usually deliver the goods within 24 hours. This makes sense with orders up to 300 CDs, or when the CDs are in cardboard sleeves. Larger orders are handled by forwarding agencies, who normally take around two days to deliver. On the first day, the goods are normally deposited by the manufacturers at a large distribution centre in your area. The individual orders are sent out on the second day. It is also possible in some cases to pick up your CDs yourself from the distribution centre. If you prefer to do things this way, you have to discuss it with the manufacturer and the transport company.

You (or someone you trust) must be at the delivery address on the day the CDs are to be delivered. If drivers cannot hand over the goods personally, they take the goods back to the distribution centre you may be charged extra for the second delivery date.

Check the goods straight away

The driver will give you a receipt to sign, which shows you've received the delivery in perfect condition.

If you notice any damage to the goods on the pallet, such as squashed or opened boxes, you should only accept the goods with reservations or indeed reject the consignment. Ask the driver to make a note of any damage on the delivery note. If any CDs are damaged, you then have the right to claim damages.

That is why it is vital that you are there in person to sign for the goods. If the driver sees a note such as "Please leave the delivery in the garage", the goods are your responsibility from that moment on. If you later discover any damage to the goods, it is no longer the forwarding agency's responsibility, as the damage could have been caused after delivery.

▶▶ *What if anything goes wrong?*

When you have done everything you need to do and have sent all the documents to the manufacturer, you are really looking forward to getting the finished CDs back. That is what makes you feel all the more disappointed if what you get back is not what you expected. You could discover that the colours on the booklet have not come out as planned, or that the manufacturer has forgotten to shrinkwrap your CDs.

You cannot hold the manufacturer responsible for every error, of course. The quality of the finished product depends on the input material, while errors are sometimes caused by factors beyond the manufacturer's control.

All details are in the manufacturer's 'General terms and conditions'. What follows is a summary of the most common points.

Responsibility for material
'The company is not responsible for master media received. In case of loss or accidental damage on the part of the company, only the cost of replacements will be refunded.'

You may have seen a disclaimer like this one at a photo lab. If the film is accidentally damaged, the cost price of a replacement is all you can claim. This always applies, regardless of whether the film contained photographs by an extremely expensive professional photographer, or whether it had a precious snapshot on it. It is not possible to claim for any losses other than material ones. If a CD master gets accidentally damaged, or a DAT gets accidentally wiped, the material costs are all you will be refunded. That is why it is vital you keep a back-up copy of the audio master and copies of your files for film output stored somewhere safe.

Delayed delivery

'Delivery dates are not binding. The company is not responsible for damage arising from deliveries which arrive too late. Neither are customers entitled to cancel orders as a result of delayed deliveries'.

There is a reason manufacturers use the phrase 'planned delivery time' when letting customers know when goods are due to arrive. Even when the finished goods leave the manufacturer's premises on time, there is no guarantee customers will get them on time. Transport companies' lorries can break down, or the pallet can be delivered to the wrong address by mistake. If your delivery does then arrive a day late, you have no right to claim damages. What's more, you can no longer cancel the order.

If you have been given a delivery date by a manufacturer, you can usually rely on the goods arriving around that date. Delays are more likely to occur during transportation, as lots of outside influences play a part. As so many things can arise to cause complications, it is sensible to allow one or two extra days. It is quite embarrassing to throw a CD release party without a CD!

Misprints in the booklet and on the inlay card

'The customer is to send in the necessary documents for printing the booklets and the inlay card as well as the CD label in perfect condition. Responsibility for print quality can only be accepted when a colour proof or Cromalin is received.'

Pictures always look different on a screen to on paper. Even inkjet or colour laser printers do not show colours the same as when they are offset printed. Manufacturers' printing machines are regularly calibrated so the print in the booklet should look exactly as it does in the documents you have sent in. These, however, do not always look like they do on your computer screen. If the colours are important, then a proof or Cromalin is a good idea.

Proofs help to avoid nasty shocks

You can get proofs made in your repro studio before the films are run. If the colours come out exactly as you expect them to, the film output can go ahead. If you are not happy with the proofs, you can delay the output until you have made all the necessary changes.

When manufacturers receive your documents, it is a big help to their printers if a proof is enclosed. They then have something to guide them when making small adjustments to their machines and can then get as close as possible to the colours you want.

If something still goes wrong with the printing

If there is a too big difference between the printed booklet or label and the proof you enclosed, the manufacturer can be held responsible. You can either negotiate a discount, or insist they do the printing again at no extra cost.

Audio material on CD-R

'All audio material sent in must have been checked by the customer and be ready for transferring'

When the glass master is being made, the only checks made on the audio material are technical ones. If there are too many errors in a row on the CD master, the glass mastering process will be stopped. This is very rare, but if it happens, you have to generate a new CD master and send it to the manufacturer. Any crackles or dropouts on the material will not necessarily be picked up during the glass mastering process, and the manufacturer cannot be held responsible. That is why it is advisable to listen to the CD master one last time before sending it to the manufacturer in particular. You should listen for noise during the spaces between songs.

If there is an error on the finished CDs which is not on the CD master, then it is the manufacturer's fault. They will, of course, do the CDs again at their own expense.

Other points

You will receive an order confirmation from the manufacturer which you should check through carefully, as it is the basis of your work together. If you have stated on your order that the CDs should be shrinkwrapped, this should appear on the confirmation. Contact the manufacturer if things like this have been missed. The same thing applies, of course, to the size of the booklet or any special features.

You can complain if your CDs are not shrinkwrapped, when it was specifically mentioned in your order and the manufacturer's confirmation, and seek a discount or you can return the CD's for shrinkwrapping at the manufacturers cost.

CHAPTER 4

▶▶ Checklists

*These checklists will help you keep a close eye
on each step involved in the making of the CD,
and keep tabs on what you still have to do.*

You can find out about

▶▶ **Audio masters**

▶▶ **Artwork for film output**

▶▶ **Layout-data for the technician doing the film
output or the manufacturer**

▶▶ **Checking films for printing**

▶▶ **Manufacturer/Replicator**

▶▶ **MCPS and legal questions**

▶▶ **Your order**

In the checklists you will find a summary of the important steps involved in manufacturing a CD

You should photocopy these pages before starting work and go through them several times so you're aware of the things you need to do. When you have started work, you can tick off all the things you have already done. You won't forget anything and will avoid possible hold-ups.

▶▶ Audio masters

☐ A high-quality CD-R has been used to generate the CD master.

☐ The CD-R looks in good condition, has no scratches and is free of dust and dirt.

☐ The CD-R has been listened to all the way through, checked for crackles and other errors.

☐ The skip button has been used to check that the starting points correspond to the start of each song.

☐ A soft marker has been used to write the titles, band name and catalogue number etc. on to the CD-R.

☐ The CD-R is in a jewel case and has been protected for transporting.

▶▶ Artwork for film output

☐ The specification measurements have been followed precisely.

☐ The trim marks and bleed have been included on the layout for the inlay card, booklet etc.

☐ All the necessary logos have been included for printing the label.

☐ No trim marks or bleed have been given for the CD label.

☐ The booklet pages have been assembled in the right order (e.g. 8+1, 2+7, 6+3, 4+5 for an eight-page booklet).

☐ All the pictures and images used have a resolution of 300 dpi/120 cpi or more.

☐ All colour pictures are in CMYK mode and all black/white pictures are in grey scales.

☐ All special colours used (e.g. for a red logo) have been converted into CMYK.

☐ Printouts have been made of the documents and have been checked through thoroughly.

▶▶ *Layout-data for the technician doing the film output or the manufacturer*

☐ Whichever data carrier is used (CD, ZIP, JAZZ etc.), the technician has everything they need, including:

    ☐ All files for printing.

    ☐ All pictures used.

    ☐ All the fonts used.

    ☐ The manufacturer's specifications.

☐ All explanations and instructions are enclosed, or have been discussed (e.g. booklet with 60 point screen, CMYK, offset / label print with 40 point screen, black/white, screen print etc. – the technician can also get this information from the manufacturer's specifications).

☐ The format of the data has been discussed with the reproduction studio or the manufacturer.

▶▶ *Checking films for printing*

☐ All necessary details including page numbers, have been written on the film (4 films per colour page/1 film per black/white page).

☐ The films have been compared with the corrected printouts (and final alterations made).

☐ The films for printing the CD label are silk screen films (unless a four colour label is required).

☐ The films for printing inlay cards, booklets etc. have trim marks.

☐ Cutting marks and crosshair marks are on all films.

☐ The films are not damaged or bent.

☐ The films are packed in a roll or with a layer of cardboard so they cannot be bent or creased.

▶▶ *Manufacturer/Replicator*

☐ The manufacturer has made a definite offer.

☐ You have informed your manufacturer about your order.

☐ You have the manufacturer's address.

☐ You have discussed the delivery deadlines.

☐ The material to be sent to the manufacturer contains:

    ☐ All of the films.

    ☐ The CD-R.

    ☐ An order form or letter.

    ☐ A telephone number in case of queries.

▶▶ *MCPS and legal questions*

☐ Your registration with MCPS has been agreed with the manufacturer.

☐ The MCPS list has been filled in.

☐ Royalties have been cleared (only with compilation CDs containing other artists).

☐ Cover versions have been cleared.

▶▶ *Your order*

☐ Order confirmation received and checked.

☐ Any deposit required paid.

☐ Goods delivered in good condition.

☐ Nothing is missing from the order.

CHAPTER 5

►►Crucial sales strategies for your CD

When you receive your finished CD from the manufacturer, the second part of your work begins: selling and advertising.

'Sales strategies for your CD' gives an insight into distribution channels – retailers and Internet – and shows ways to go about promoting your CD, even on a low budget.

You can find out about:
- ►► *Working with a professional distributor*
- ►► *Promotion and marketing strategies*
- ►► *Applying to labels and concert organisers*
- ►► *Sales and promotion over the Internet*

▶▶ Working with a professional distributor

A music distributor's representative is visiting the purchasing manager of a CD store in Manchester. "I've got Madonna's latest CD, a Beatles compilation and the début CD by the band X from Southampton." The purchasing manager will snap up the Madonna and Beatles CDs, which are easy to sell, but will think, why should a music fan in Manchester buy a CD by an unknown band from Southampton. He will not take any CDs by band X unless there's a label behind them with all the marketing and promotion that goes with it. He does not have enough space in his shop to give this newcomer a chance.

If magazines are running advertisements for the band, or if a local tour and radio performances are coming up, then the purchasing manager might be prepared to put one or two CDs by an unknown artist in his shop. That does not mean to say that the CDs are as good as sold. The outlet buys on a sale-or-return basis, and can send goods back to the distributors if they are not sold within a certain time.

You can do it better
Look for a professional distributor. As another option, you should ask yourself whether you could organise the distribution yourself, and (what is more important) do a better job.

Applying to a distributor
Only look for a professional distributor if you are prepared to invest a lot of time and money in your music. Before you try to sell your music in stores further afield, there has to be a real chance that someone will buy it.

Sales forecasts will tell distributors which bands and labels to include in their catalogue.

The music plays a part in their choice, of course, but even the best song does not sell itself. When you are trying to sell your CD to a distributor, it has to be accompanied by a marketing and promotion plan.

A convincing marketing plan
The marketing plan includes details about advertising, as well as everything else aimed at getting people to buy the CD. This includes advertisements in music, city or lifestyle magazines, posters and radio advertising. If a tour is planned to promote the album, this has to be included in the marketing plan.

The promotion is more important than marketing
The promotion plan includes all 'unpaid' activities such as making time to give an interview or to have your CD reviewed in a magazine, doing a promotion concert for the press or getting air time on radio for the CD.

This information is important for the distributor. Their representative might not convince purchasing managers with the quality of the music but can emphasise sales potential.

How do you find the right distributor?
When looking for possible distributors, look for artists that play a similar style of music to yours. You will find details of their distributors on the inlay cards. You should only focus your attention on the smaller distributors as, even if you do manage to end up with a major company, your chances of high sales are slim. Representatives of large record companies will always give preference to their company's own CDs when presenting their products to stores.

You have a much better chance if you decide on a smaller distributor as you will not be competing with megastars.

How distributors work
There is little difference in the way the various distributors operate. CDs are only ever accepted from small labels or newcomers on a commission basis.

You are only paid for a CD when it is sold. CDs not sold within a certain time are sent back.

The distributor will give you a share of the income amounting to around 10% per CD sold. The following diagram shows how the proceeds from a £10 CD might be divided up, with small quantities the manufacturing element will be much higher:

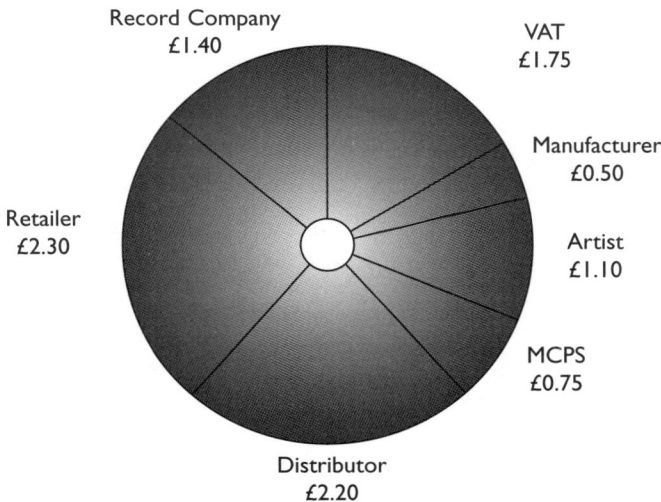

Record Company £1.40

VAT £1.75

Manufacturer £0.50

Retailer £2.30

Artist £1.10

MCPS £0.75

Distributor £2.20

What does a distributor do?

A distributor does not assume responsibility for production costs or do any advertising. You are responsible for all costs involved in the making of the finished product, as well as marketing and promotion.

As well as the CDs themselves, the distributor needs product information in a 'sales sheet', which it sends to the retailer to give the purchasing manager information about a new CD in advance.

The sales sheet contains the following details:

Record label, distributor, release date, the CD's EAN-code and catalogue number, the telephone and fax numbers of the distributor for orders, and a picture of the cover, as well as planned marketing and promotion. If space allows, you can include information about the band, a photo of the musicians and a list of the songs.

The way to apply to a distributor is exactly the same as for a record company. You can find tips on how to do this on page 68.

Organising the distribution yourself

Gigs are a good way for newcomers to distribute their CDs. If you can convince your audience with a live performance, they will also be interested in a CD.

Look around for mail order firms. That is the surest way to reach your target audience. Customers who order CDs by mail order are usually interested in music and are more likely to risk buying something by an unknown newcomer than those who wander around stores in shopping centres. You can send the mail order company one of your CDs as a sample and suggest a deal on a commission basis. If you also offer the CD at a good price of say £5-£6.00 a distributor can sell it for £12.00 in their catalogue. This means your CD sells for less than average, which is another incentive for customers to buy it.

Take the CDs to the retailer yourself

Use the advantage of being cheaper than the competition. If you have a distributor, a copy of your CD will be just one among many in the shop, possibily all on sale for the price of £10 or more. If it is not sold within three to six months, it goes back to the distributor.

When launching a CD, stock the local shops yourself. You can offer them the CDs on a commission basis and give ten or fifteen copies a prime position in the shop. This way, you cut out the middleman and can get £4 to £5 for each CD sold. The retailer can then sell them on for £7 to £8 each. That may significantly increase the chances of your CD being sold.

▶▶ *Promotion and marketing strategies*

With most independent productions, the time spent in the studio and the manufacture of the CDs swallows up the whole budget. If you have money left over, however, think about how best to invest it.

Cleverly thought-out marketing, from the design of the CD to an elaborate advertising campaign, is normal with large record companies but impossible for you. That is why you should focus on your strong points and compensate for the low budget with maximum commitment.

Even if you put an advertisement in a magazine, it will achieve relatively little. No-one will buy a CD by a band they have never heard of just because of an advertisement.

The power of the press
Though an article in a magazine does not cost anything it might have a lot more influence on readers than an advertisement. Don't just send the CD in to a magazine, and ring up and ask who is responsible for coverage of your type of music, and direct your CD to named people.

If a journalist writes something about your CD, you have already achieved your first success. But you do not have to leave it at that. Let them know about everything else your band does and invite the writer to a gig. If he likes your performance, he might very well follow up with a live report.

Promoting a CD is a very intricate process. You should take every opportunity to attract people's attention. If a gig is coming up in a particular town, you can invite the local radio station to offer some of your CDs or free tickets in their prize draw. Invite the music editor of the local newspapers.

Use every way possible to get yourselves noticed.

Whatever you do, keep cool!
Don't panic if you get a bad press. Everyone's taste is different and a bad press is still better than no reaction at all.

▶▶ Applying to labels and concert organisers

Finding the right label
Use the same method to find a record company as a distributor. You will find label details on your favourite CDs together with a telephone number or a web address where you can find more information. Advertisements for new releases in magazines and fanzines are another source of information.

Try to find a contact person with the label
Before applying to a particular record label, you have to make sure the material arrives with the right person.

An application without naming a contact person is pointless, especially with larger companies. Even if headquarters pass the CD to an A&R manager, they are not likely to pass it on to the person who deals with your type of music. An A&R manager in a record company always looks after a certain style. In a major record company there are A&R managers for jazz, hiphop, rock, pop and heavy metal. Phone the record company and ask to be put through to the person responsible for your style of music. Your application is then more personal, which helps to arouse interest.

Use the A&R manager's name when you write
Mention your earlier phone call. If you are lucky, the A&R manager will remember the call and pay more attention to your application.

Keep the letter short, as the A&R manager does not have a lot of time. Mention your CD and the enclosed information about the band. In addition, you should make it clear why you have sent the material to the company: you like the repertoire of that particular label and would like them to bring out your next recording.

You can also let them know you will be phoning again to ask for feedback about your CD. Even if you are unsuccessful, it is still worth getting an opinion and tips from a professional, which can help in your future work.

Keep it brief
The information you send about the band should include a picture of the musicians and be concise. Ten lines are enough. No A&R manager has the time to read a page of band information.

Leave out the things which are unimportant. It doesn't matter to the A&R manager whether a guitarist left the band two years ago due to "personal differences", or whether you reached third place in a youth club band contest.

Include things such as how long the band has been working together, whether you have brought out any recordings, how many gigs you have played in the past few years and whether any of them were supporting well-known bands.

Accentuate the positive
Show A&R managers how seriously you take things and that they can rely on your full commitment in the future. You can also include some excerpts from positive write-ups. Whatever you do, do not include lengthy extracts from newspapers. One or two sentences and the source are enough:

"One of the best indie-rock newcomers this year. Rarely has a British band demonstrated so impressively that good guitar rock does not have to come from the States."
NME 4/2002

Make sure when you put the application together that everything is clear, informative and not too wordy. Write the name of the band and other details on the CD and the photo, and don't forget to include a correspondence address, telephone number and email address. The way the application looks must grab attention and be consistent. When trying to convince an A&R manager that you are a quality act, good music is only half the battle. An application prepared in an interesting way is also vital.

How do you book a gig?
The first question for organisers is whether the band has enough potential and is well-known enough to fill a club or a hall.

You can find clubs and gig venues in music magazines as well as details of upcoming tours. You can get the addresses and telephone numbers of the promoters over the Internet, or from directory enquiries. As with applications to record companies, all the contact you make with concert promoters should be personal.

Applications to a concert promoter are the same as applications to a record label.

Enclose a CD, some information about the band and a photo. It is also important to a promoter whether you are doing all the advertising and having all the posters made for the gig or the tour. Advertising does not necessarily involve expensive advertisements in the press. When organising a gig in a club, a good promotion job can be done very cheaply with a bit of effort. You can organise a presentation or local radio interview and get better results than with an advertisement in the press. Send in a few CDs or free tickets to the radio station for their prize draw. That will give the station a good reason to include you in their programme and help arouse interest.

A local band is an advantage
If you are not known in a particular town, appearing with a local support band is a good idea. Local bands have a steady following of fans who will always come to the concert. The organisers are then guaranteed a certain audience size and you know you will not be turning up to play in an empty hall.

▶▶ *Sales and promotion over the Internet*

The music industry is complaining of losses running into many millions through illegal CD copying and MP3 files downloaded from the Internet. This affects well-established bands the most, but can present you with a good opportunity. While you cannot sell more CDs over the Internet, you do have a chance to become better-known.

Your own web page
Web surfers can listen to some of your songs on your website, without any obligation to buy. If they like your material, you will have gained a new fan who may well come to a gig or buy a CD in the future.

Sound on the net
The two most popular file formats for music on the Internet are Real Audio and MP3. Real Audio is a streaming process. The audio data is highly compressed and can be played in real time straight from the server. The user then does not have to wait while the data is being downloaded and can carry on surfing whilst listening to the song. Information about the player and compressing can be found on the Real web site at http://www.real.co.uk

The MP3 format is recommended

The audio data is compressed to around one tenth of their original size and can be downloaded by the user. They then have the sound file on their computer's hard disk and can listen to it on an MP3 player, as well as recording it on to CD or MD. You can find information about MP3 at http://www.mp3.com

Though other audio formats exist on the Internet, MP3 and Real Audio are the most important. The Internet user is sure to have a piece of software on their computer they can use to play them.

As well as sound files, you can also use your web pages to sell CDs or various types of merchandise.

You can reach a wide audience through music websites (portals)

Have a look at the home pages of www.vitaminic.com or www.besonic.com These put your songs on the net so people can download them either free or for a fee. There are systems where people can vote for their favourite newcomer. You will find plenty of opportunities like these on the net. Take advantage of as many as possible and make your songs available.

The first thing to do is to make a name for yourselves. This will make the task of selling your CDs a whole lot easier.

CHAPTER 6

▶▶Choosing ISRC and EAN codes

Find out about:

▶▶ *ISRC codes are available for every production*

▶▶ *The EAN/bar code is important if you want your CD to be sold in the shops*

▶▶ *The three parts to an EAN code*

▶▶ *ISRC codes are available for every production*

The ISRC code was introduced as early as 1986 to make it possible to identify music digitally. This is for checking purposes. Whenever recordings are put on the internet or digitally broadcast, the ISRC code is included, although it cannot be heard on the recording.

This means that it is possible for ISRC codes to replace label codes, as soon as radio stations switch over to digital broadcasts. Stations would be able to keep track of play lists digitally and it would also ensure that royalties are distributed fairly.

How can you get an ISRC code?
The ISRC is assigned by the Internation ISRC Agency. It is free and you don't need to have a catalogue number at the time of recording.

When is the ISRC put together?
CDs are given a code at the premastering stage and an ISRC code is put before each song on request in mastering studios. A lot of professional mastering tools, such as the "Masterlist CD" software by Digidesign can be used to assign ISRC codes. This is included in a CD's PQ data, which also contain the starting point, the playing time and other information relevant to the CD.

The ISRC code is divided up into four parts:
ISRC GB-P55-97-00001

GB - The country code. It stands for the country in which the recording's owner is based. Each country always has two letters.

P55 - Registrant code. Each firm or band can be identified through a three-character code.

97 - Year of reference. This gives the year the recording was made, and is assigned by the owner.

00001 - Designation code. The owner of the ISRC gives each song its own number. In our example, a CD with 12 songs would have GB-P55-0001 for song 1, GB-P55-00002 for song 2 etc, up to GB-P55-97-00012 for the last song.

If you make a second CD, the numbering will simply be continued.

You can get further information from the following address:
International ISRC Agency
c/o IFPI Secretariat
54 Regent Street
London W1B 5RE
Tel: 020 7878 7900
Fax: 020 7878 7950
email: philippa.morell@ifpi.org

▶▶ The EAN/bar code is important if you want your CD to be sold in the shops

The EAN (European Article Number) is a standardised numbering system used for generating bar codes for recording sales with electronic cash registers.

Every product available in shops should have an EAN bar code. As well as the large chain stores, more and more small music shops are switching over to electronic tills.

EANs are assigned by:
e.centre
Maltravers Street 10
London WC2R 3BX
Tel: 020 7655 9000
Fax: 020 7681 2290
email: info@e-centre.org.uk
web site: www.e-centre.org.uk

Membership of the e-centre makes it possible for you to have your own EAN codes generated for your CD. Membership is relatively expensive, however. A one-off membership fee is as high as the yearly fee, and is based on the turnover you make with all your productions each year. With a turnover of up to £500,000, the yearly contribution is £85 (01/01/2002). This means it is not worth joining just for one production. A lot of manufacturers are members, however, and are therefore able to assign EAN codes themselves. This makes it far cheaper for you than if you join yourself. Manufacturers and brokers often assign an EAN code for around £15-30.

▶▶ *There are three parts to an EAN bar code*

An example:

40 = the first two digits give the country code
31917 = the company prefix number. Each member is identified through a five-digit number.
000759 = the individual item reference and a checking digit.

A few manufacturers send an EAN code already encoded as a picture or as a vector file, which enables you to integrate it directly into the layout of your design. The best place for it is on the back inlay card. Otherwise you can generate the bar code on your own computer using shareware available on the internet. Find this by entering words such as EAN and UPC into a search engine.

What information does an EAN contain?

The EAN bar code does not include any information in the encoding. other than the number. The number assigned is unique, so no other product in Europe will have the same code. If the EAN code contained price information from the time it was coded, then the product would have to cost the same everywhere!

The information is individually assigned

If a newly-released CD comes into the shops, the EAN number is entered into the cash registers. If the register comes up with "EAN unknown", the store's purchasing manager enters the information into his register system, which appears when the CD is swiped over the electronic till reader. He enters the name of the artist, the title of the CD and the price. The EAN information is assigned from that moment on, although it is limited to that one shop or chain.

If the CD is to be sold only at gigs, there is no point in giving it an EAN. As soon as the CD is put on sale in shops, however, an EAN code is very advisable as many retailers will not accept products without bar codes.

Bringing out a CD abroad

EANs are also a good idea when bringing out a CD in other European countries. As the name "European Article Number" already implies, this is standard all over Europe.

The American equivalent to the EAN code is the UPC (Uniform Product Code). UPCs can only be assigned in the USA and only have a point if the CD in question is to be sold in the USA. UPCs are not compatible with EANs.

CHAPTER 7

▶▶ Legal questions relating to CD production

Whether you are including cover versions on your CD, putting together as a sampler with other bands or registering the name of your band as a protected trademark, you have to know the legal stumbling blocks.

Learn about the following:

▶▶ *Copyright – how do you protect your music?*

▶▶ *Protect your band name*

▶▶ *Cutting cover versions*

▶▶ *Sampler/Compilation CDs*

▶▶ *Different types of music business contract*

▶▶ *Copyright – how do you protect your music?*

The current charts show that there is no better way into the pop music industry for a newcomer band than through a TV show. The pop group Liberty X for example, owes their success to the programme 'Pop Idol' even though they were nominally a failure on the show. Several current pop stars have enjoyed great success after appearing in Neighbours (the Australian TV Soap).

When you have written a pop song for such a type of TV-format, send your application to producers of films and TV series. As a rule, you should prepare yourself for a rejection. The amount of material sent in is very high, and the song has to fit in with the idea of the show.

What can you do, though, when you switch on the TV a year later and hear your song, which you thought had been rejected? You can sue the producers for pinching your song and having another artist record it. In cases like these, however, it is up to you to prove it.

It does not matter in this case that you have registered your song with the MCPS. The important thing is that you are the originator of the song and have to prove it. All the songs you compose are automatically copyright. If you wrote the song together with other people, then you are all originators of the song, the co-originators.

How can you protect your work?
You can do this using the postal service. Wrap up the CD in an envelope which cannot be opened without tearing it and send it to yourself by recorded delivery. When you receive the envelope the day after, just store it away in a safe place. If you do have to go to court, you will be able to prove beyond all doubt when you composed the song. The envelope will be presented to the judge, who will be able to see clearly that the package is unopened. The postmark should also show the judge when it was sent. It is up to individual judges, though, whether this can be accepted as evidence, which means this solution is far from ideal.

There is a second (and safer) possibility. Deposit the CD with a solicitor. Depositing a CD costs upwards of £40, depending on how much it is valued at. This investment could turn out to be worthwhile.

Neither way, however, guarantees that the originator will win the case outlined above. The final decision rests with the judge, who has to decide whether the 'stolen' version is the same as the originator's original and the outcome is impossible to predict.

Do you really have to deposit a copy of every song?
A band applying to a record label with a rock music CD can spare themselves all this effort. The record company is not likely to take a rock song and give it to another band to record. If, however, you compose for a pop singer whose songs are written by professionals, it is vital to deposit your work with a solicitor.

►► Protect your band name

It is often more difficult to find a name for the band than it is to write your own songs. Even after you have found a good name for your band, you may not be allowed to use it. Lots of bands have had to change their name, as there were already artists using the same or a similar name.

Liberty X were originally just called Liberty. The problem was, this name was already in use. "JBO" started out as the "James Blast Orchestra", but had to change their name, as there was too much danger of confusion with the original "James Last Orchestra".

Legal disputes over the name of bands are not uncommon. It is difficult to generalise, as the right to a name is very complex.

Where can you register band names?
If you have a good name for your band, it is worth getting it registered. In the UK, this is done through the patents office in South Wales. At the Internet address www.patent.gov.uk you will find application forms and further information. At the time of writing, they charge £200 per patent. Getting a name registered takes around six months. Your band's name is then patented for ten years after the registration date. You can also extend the patent when it runs out.

Contact:
The Patent Office Trade Marks Registry
Cardiff Road, Newport, South Wales. NP10 8QQ
Tel: 08159 500 505. Fax: 01633 813 600.
Email: enquiries@patent.gov.uk
Internet: www.patent.gov.uk

▶▶ *Cutting cover versions*

'Heartbreak Hotel' was Elvis Presley's first chart success. He recorded the single in 1955 for the RCA record company. It was released in February 1956, and the single went platinum in November 1957, which means it had sold over a million copies. The songs which followed, 'Don't Be Cruel', 'Hound Dog' and 'Love Me Tender', also went platinum. All these songs were cover versions, and their original versions (e.g. 'Love Me Tender', originally by Vera Matson) are hardly known today. All those involved have profited from these releases. Presley became famous and made money through royalties from the sale of the singles and LPs. The songs' original composers made money from the distribution of authors' royalties.

Even today, bands still use the possibility of drawing attention to themselves through cover versions. Legally, there is nothing to stop people doing that, or bringing these cover versions out on CD. If you do that, there are two things you must look out for:

1. MCPS
You have to pay MCPS royalties to the original composer. This happens automatically when a CD is brought out, because of the licence contract to MCPS. You put down the original composer of the song and the lyrics, and they then get a share of the MCPS royalties.

2. You must keep as close as possible to the original version
You are not allowed to make sweeping changes to a song. Changing the tempo or the instrumentation is no problem. The moment you start making changes to the arrangement or the lyrics, however, you have to get permission from the originators or their record company. Permission is necessary, even if you only leave out a chorus or change around parts of the song. You cannot change the lyrics at all. You even have to get permission to translate the lyrics.

Most of the time, the name of the publisher is on the original CD. If it is not, you can get it from MCPS. You will find the address and telephone number in chapter 6, on page 75.

You should always get permission to change a cover song
Making a punk number out of Frank Sinatra's 'My Way' at a youth club concert will not get anyone into any real trouble for failing to get permission from the publisher concerned. If the song appears on an independently-produced CD, things are very different. Even then, however, it is unlikely that the CD will fall into the hands of the original publisher's legal team.

But what happens when the CD is reviewed in an international music magazine and is full of praise for the "My Way cover version with the amusing street lyrics." The publishers are then very likely to find out about it.

Something like this can have serious consequences, from having the CDs destroyed to damages.

When producing a small number of CDs, it is almost impossible to get permission to rework a song
Unfortunately, it is difficult to get permission to rework a cover version. You have to record your version and send it to the publisher, together with a copy of the lyrics.

The publisher then has to sort everything out with the company involved in making the original version, which involves a lot of work. That is why partner companies often say no to this kind of request. If only a small number of CDs are going to be produced, the company will not get enough proceeds through the (MCPS) royalties. The amount of work involved in reworking the song is not worth it.

Do not bother with cover versions, if you are changing a version without permission. There is no problem, however, with doing a cover version which is like the original song.

▶▶ *Sampler/Compilation CDs*

On compilations (also called samplers), various bands present themselves to a wide audience. It does not matter whether it is "Bravo-Hits", the world's most successful and best-selling compilation, or a "Young Newcomer of the Year" presentation CD. The basic idea is always the same: to introduce a wide spectrum of bands or musicians to as wide an audience as possible.

A few legal questions
At the planning stage you have to contact the bands or their record labels and let them know about the sampler. You should introduce the project straight away, the first time you contact them, and give them details about the following things: Why is the compilation CD being made?

One example could be a CD for a live festival, where all the bands involved are asked to contribute one song. Another possibility could be an advertising CD for a firm, which is sent to all customers as a Christmas present.

▶ How many CDs are being made?

▶ How much will the CD be sold for?

▶ Where will the CD be available?

▶ How many bands have already been asked? Have any already said yes?

What happens next depends on the kind of compilation you are making. There are three different categories:

Commercial compilations.
Compilations with well-known bands from all over the country, made for non-commercial purposes. Commercial compilations, which are made either to be sold or as advertising material for agencies and businesses.

Regional or underground compilations
This refers to samplers like those made by clubs, to introduce bands from a particular area. Samplers can also be made with songs by bands from all over the country, giving an overview of newcomers within a certain style of music.

Bands which appear on these samplers do not already have a contract with a big record label. That makes communicating with them relatively easy, as you do not have to negotiate detailed contracts with them and you have direct contact with the musicians.

Financing a compilation
As these CDs are made on a small budget, bands normally contribute their songs free of charge. After all, they profit from being included on a compilation CD. Sometimes bands even have to pay a share of the production costs in return for having their song included on the CD. A band should be given enough free copies of the CD to sell and get back what they have invested.

Get a contract drawn up
Put at least the important points in writing. You need to have full rights of use to the songs to include them on the CD. The contract sets out how much each band has to pay, as well as other things such as free copies of the CD or royalties.

You should agree to transfer the rights of use to songs with compilations on a non-exclusive basis. That gives you the right to use a song on the compilation, though the band can still bring out the song themselves. You can of course sign an exclusive contract, if the song has been composed specifically for your sampler, that forbids the band to bring out the song themselves for the duration of the contract.

Compilations with well-known bands

You could make the CD to give away with a magazine, or as part of a music festival to sell as an entrance ticket. CDs like these may very well include famous bands which are under contract with large record companies. Their labels, of course, only give permission for a song to be used on the CD if it is to their or the artists' advantage, either through royalty payments or extra publicity.

How do you obtain the licence rights?

You do not earn any money if you enclose the CD free in a magazine or give it out at a concert, so you have to persuade the record companies of the publicity value for the bands on the CD.

If you make a CD for a festival, it gives those who go the chance to have another look at the bands they have seen. They will then remember the bands or songs they liked best and buy a complete CD later on. CDs in magazines have a similar effect. Readers can read about a band and then listen to the CD. These arguments are often enough to get free permission to include a song.

A contract with a major label

The licensing contracts come from the legal departments of the large record companies and cover the following points:

▶ Exactly how many copies of the compilation CD are going to be produced. The maximum sales price and where the CD will be distributed. In the case of a festival CD, there will be a clause in the contract stating that you may only distribute the CD at the festival and not sell it later through retailers.

▶ How long the CD will be on sale for and whether distribution will be limited to the festival or to one edition of a magazine.

▶ Which details will be given in the booklet about the originator and the person or company with the exploitation rights. This could include the record company's address, the publisher, details about the composer and the lyrics.

▶ The guarantee that the CD will be licenced by MCPS.

▶ Commercial compilations which are to be sold or used as advertising material for a company.

▶ If a compilation CD is used for commercial purposes, royalty payments are due to the record companies. There compilation CDs can therefore be divided into two types:

1. CDs which are sold in stores

With CDs which are sold in stores, the published price to dealer determines the royalties paid. The published price to dealer (PPD) is the average sales price at which the distributor sells the goods to retailers. This amounts to around £6-8 net for CDs in the normal price range. As a rule, the royalties amount to around 15-20% of the PPD for the whole CD. In the case of a compilation CD with ten songs by different bands, each band gets 1.5-2%. That means royalties of £0.09 - £0.12 for each CD sold if the PPD is £6.

It is only worthwhile for the record company if a certain minimum number of CDs are sold. If you are intending to produce 1,000 copies, they will simply say no straight away, as there is too much trouble and effort involved for so little expected profit.

2. CDs used as advertising

Royalties are worked out slightly differently in the case of CDs used for advertising. The first thing companies do is to fix an imaginary PPD, as in the case of CDs for stores. Then, they add on a fee of around £0.30 and £1.25 per CD. That way, they get paid because their music is used in the advertising.

As with a compilation CD, the royalties only become interesting for record companies if a large number of CDs are produced. The consent of the record company also depends on whether the artist is prepared to endorse the product being advertised.

▶▶ Different types of music business contract

A contract with a record company is the basis for the work you do together in the future. That is why you should look at it very, very carefully and go through it point by point with a lawyer. The Musicians Union offers an alternative. Members can send them copies of contracts, which they then have checked by lawyers specialising in the music business. For more information on the Musicians Union see page 90.

Contracts cover more than just recordings
Contracts are not just limited to music for a CD-release. Normally, artists give up all other rights associated with the recording. This includes making money from T-shirts, stickers and other fan merchandise as well as the exploitation of videos and films about the band. The record company gains the right to use your work as film music or for making commercials. Other things included in a recording contract are clauses about support tours or advertising appearances. Individual points are a matter for negotiation and you should get advice from a lawyer.

There are two possible types of contract for an artist: a record takeover agreement or an Artist deal.

The record takeover agreement:
This contract refers to tapes by a music group. The term is a bit old fashioned, as recordings are no longer handed over on tape. The right name for it would be a "CD delivery contract".

In the case of a record takeover agreement the record company's main responsibility comes after the recording and mastering. The artist delivers the finished audio material to the record company. This means that with a record takeover agreement you have a lot of freedom as an artist. It begins with the choice of recording studio and producer and includes the choice of which songs to record and which order they come on the CD as well as the mastering.

Who finances the recording?
The recordings are fully or partially funded by an advance from the record company. The advance is deducted from the royalties which the artist receives from sales of the recording. If the artist finances a part of the recording from their own pocket, it means less of a risk for the record company. On the other hand, the artist gets a higher share of the profits, calculated from the PPD.

What do you get as the artist?

The usual share of the profits with a record takeover agreement is about 14-18% of the PPD. If the PPD is £10, the artist's share of the profits is between £1.40 and £1.80.

One particular feature of a record takeover agreement is that the artist is responsible for paying part of the cost of videos and tour support. If a video is made and the production costs come to £40,000, the artist has to pay 50%. The amount is given to the artist as an advance but, once again, deducted from the royalties later.

One advantage for the artist is that it is not the artist's problem if the single is a flop and the royalties do not cover the cost of the advance. The artist does not have to pay back part of the investment in this case. The risk is the record company's.

The same thing applies to tour support

If a record company books a newcomer as tour support for a well-known act, then the company has to bear part of the cost of financing the tour. Few people will come to listen to a warm-up act. The main act is what fills up halls, but the support act still needs accommodation in a hotel or bus, food, a sound engineer and stagehands.

The support act's record company has to help finance these expenses. As with making a video, both the company and the artist share the costs fifty-fifty, but the record label puts up all of the money in advance.

Negotiate the length of the agreement

It could include the production of one album, or up to four or five. The record company will normally offer you a contract for one or two albums. In addition, the company will make sure it has the right of option. If you sign up for one CD with two options, the label can extend the contract twice for a further album. The conditions of the original contract apply to the options, too.

Sign up for as few options as possible.

Only the record company can ask for the inclusion of options. The artist has no right to object to one and cannot insist on one, either. If the first two albums a band made are flops, there is no way the company will want to exercise an option. If the band is successful, though, the company will insist on one and the contract will be extended. That can be a disadvantage for the artist. They have accepted a bad contract at the start of their career, just to be given a chance but only when is it possible for the artist to negotiate a better contract.

The Artist deal

With an artist deal, the record company accepts all the costs. This has advantages as well as disadvantages. One crucial advantage is that it involves no financial input at all from the artist. The record company pays for the studio, the producer, videos and tours. On the other hand, the musicians only have a limited say in everything. The record company could commission outside composers to write songs for the artists, choose the producer and the studio and decide which songs go on an album and which are released as singles. Since the artists do not invest any money, they get fewer royalties. The artist's share of the profits amounts to 4-8% of the PPD.

Artist deals are normal for chart music

Record companies sign Artist deals with bands they want to spend a lot of time and effort on, to get them to the top. Boy-bands, for example, have Artist deals. Record takeover agreements are standard in the case of rock music, or with small record companies. Artist deals are signed for a minimum of three years, with the record company normally reserving the right of option for a long time afterwards. A lot of work goes into establishing the artist and they stay tied to the company.

CHAPTER 8

►► # Associations and institutions

The music industry offers very few possibilities for training, help and advice. Associations are the only bodies which make it possible to exchange opinions, experiences, etc with those in the same business.

Find out about:
►► *The Musicians Union*
►► *AIM - Association of Independent Music*
►► *BPI - British Phonographic Industry*
►► *MCPS - Mechanical-Copyright Protection Society*

Music promotion in associations
There are many organisations and associations in England which are dedicated to matters musical.

▶▶ *The Musicians Union*

All musicians can become members of the Musicians Union. The membership fee is based on how much you earn from your music every year. This will be £73 for income up to £7,500. Those earning up to £15,000 from their music pay up to £112. You can expect to pay £167 if you earn up to £23,000, and those earning over £25,000 pay a membership of £220.

Members of the Musicians Union have access to a wide range of services:
▶ The MU gives all kinds of advice about the music business and is available for members to consult about legal questions.

▶ The MU regularly publishes brochures, covering topics such as copyright, managing, contracts etc, which are available to members.

▶ Trades Union representation for musicians. The MU negotiates with major employers in the TV and film business over rates of pay for musicians.

▶ The Musicians Union makes sample contracts available to its members free of charge.

▶ Access to an address file: you can enquire about the addresses of labels, concert organisers and producers.

As well as all of the above, each member receives the magazine "Musician" which comes out four times a year and covers items of interest in the music business.

Further information is available from:
Musicians Union
60-62 Clapham Road, London SW9 0JJ.
Tel: 0207 582 5566. Fax: 0207 582 9805.
email: admin@musiciansunion.org.uk
web site: www.musiciansunion.org.uk

▶▶ AIM - Association of Independent Music

The AIM was founded in February 1999. Since then their membership has grown to around 500. Independent labels, distributors and internet-labels can become members of AIM. The aim of the association is to encourage members and to assist them in their cultural tasks. AIMs membership fee is £117.50 (£100 plus 17.5% VAT).

AIM's members have the following advantages:
▶ Contacts to the foreign music industry.

▶ The possibility of taking part in seminars and events about music.

▶ Access to specialists in legal and business questions.

Further information is available from:
Lamb House, Church Street, London W4 2PD.
Tel: 020 8994 5599. Fax: 020 8994 5222.
web site: www.musicindie.org

▶▶ BPI - British Phonographic Industry

The BPI represents around 290 UK record companies. They pursue copyright issues and promote the industry to government and policy makers. Membership is based on turnover with a minimum fee of £75.00. There is also an International section which provides information on major trade fairs and exhibitions..

Further information is available from:
The British Phonographic Industry
25 Savile Row, London W1S 2ES.
Tel: 020 7851 4000. Fax 020 7851 4010.
email general@bpi.co.uk /
web site: www.bpi.co.uk

▶▶ *MCPS - Mechanical-Copyright Protection Society*

The Mechanical-Copyright Protection Society represents around 15,000 composers, songwriters and music publishers whenever their copyright musical works are recorded. Acting as an agent on behalf of its members, MCPS negotiates agreements with those who wish to record and distribute product containing copyright musical works. MCPS collects and then distributes 'mechanical' royalties generated from the copying of music on to many different formats.

MCPS membership is for writers and publishers only.

Further information is available from:
MCPS
29-33 Berners Street,
London W1T 3AB.
Tel: 0207 580 5544.
Web site: www.mcps.co.uk

CHAPTER 9

▶▶ Founding your own label

Bringing out your CD on your own label is a sensible alternative to large record companies. It gives you control over your music, and you will learn a lot more about the music business.

Find out about:
▶▶ *Getting over initial difficulties*
▶▶ *Distribution and sales*

Anybody wanting to have control over their music and the work which goes with it only has one real option: bringing out the music on their own label.

It is relatively easy to establish your own label. You should not underestimate, however, how much work is involved. You have to fight against competition from large companies and do all the work yourself.

▶▶ Getting over initial difficulties

The first step on the way to your own label is a contract either with another band, or with your own band. You then make a CD with this band. This is necessary in order to get an ISRC code. You can find information on the ISRC in chapter 6 on page 74.

Getting support and exchanging experiences as members of an association

If you are planning to bring out several CDs a year, it is worth joining the AIM. Once you have had 1,000 CDs made, you have saved enough as a AIM member to cover the cost of your annual membership fee. The AIM offers additional advantages which are particularly attractive for a new label. The AIM is described on page 91.

▶▶ Distribution and sales

Once you have a name for your label and the label code to go with it, you have overcome the bureaucratic hurdles on the way to establishing your label. Then comes your main job when running a label: selling the CDs.

Distribution presents you with your first problem. The fact that you are a small label with limited finances behind you makes it difficult for you to find a distribution partner to get your CDs in the shops. At the beginning, you need to show a lot of initiative. Start by working with small mail-order distributors who are willing to give unknown artists a chance and their sales prices are better. The CDs are offered by the label on a commission basis, so you only receive payment for goods on commission when they are sold. If a CD cannot be sold, the mail-order company can send it back to the label. Specialised websites are another distribution channel worth considering, as they give users the chance to download music using MP3, as well as the chance to order CDs directly.

Promote your CD through the press

Plan your promotion strategy for your CDs. Keep a record of the addresses of all the important music, city and lifestyle magazines, which you can use to send out applications. You can find the addresses of magazines on the Internet and telephone them to find out the names of the people to contact.

Whatever you do, never underestimate the influence small magazines and fanzines have. They are exactly what you need to reach the right target group for a small production. Fanzine readers have an above-average interest in music and have shown themselves to be more willing to buy a CD by an unknown artist.

It is also easier to work together with small magazines and fanzines, e.g. on interviews or live reports, than with established publications.

Can press advertisements help?

Promotion through reviews and articles in the press is a lot more important at the beginning than buying advertising space, which is expensive and not very effective. Music fans cannot be persuaded to buy an unknown CD through an advertisement. If, on the other hand, a journalist gives the CD a good review, it could be just what you need to get people to go out and buy it.

When you have explored all press avenues, it is time to turn your attention to radio stations. Local and music stations are your best bet. Try to work together with the station if one of your bands is on tour, offering CDs or concert tickets as prizes to get people to come to the gigs.

The things discussed here are, of course, only a small part of the work involved when you have your own label. It is difficult to make a living, so you should be motivated more by enthusiasm and idealism than the thought of making money.

CHAPTER 10

▶▶Technical details about CDs and DVDs

Misunderstandings always arise when preparing the material for a CD when no-one knows what certain technical terms mean, or which manufacturing processes are involved. This chapter describes the stages involved in the production process.

Find out about:

▶▶ *The different types of CD format*

▶▶ *The technical process of manufacturing a CD*

▶▶ *DVD – Digital Versatile Disc*

▶▶ The different types of CD format

Since CDs were introduced in 1982, various formats have been developed. Some did not take off, such as the CD-I (interactive) or the Video-CD, but many other important formats still exist.

CD-DA (Digital audio)
This is the original form of the CD. The technical specifications of audio CDs are set out in the so-called 'Red Book'. This standard states that the audio information is stored as 44,100 16-bit samples per second and there are two channels (left and right). In addition, CDs have to be written in 'Disk at Once' mode. The songs must not be written over several sessions. The CD player reads the data on a CD-DA at single speed transfer rate. (Drive speed is expressed as multiples of the single speed transfer rate, as 2x, 4x, 6x, and so on.)

This standard guarantees that each CD-DA can be read by each CD player or CD-ROM drive.

CDs have been produced for a few years now with a copy protection mechanism. Most CDs are produced with this mechanism, which makes CD-DAs unplayable in a CD-ROM drive. Their aim is to stop CDs being digitally copied on to a CD-R.

CD-ROM (Read Only Memory)
The CD-DA was extended to 'Yellow Book' specifications in 1985. This standard describes CD-ROMs, which contain computer data. Since then, the 'Yellow Book' standard has been extended to ISO 9660 standard. This ensures that all CD-ROMS are readable on every single modern operating system.

CD-Extra / Enhanced CD
The standard for the CD-Extra, also called Enhanced CD, were set out in the 'Blue Book' in 1996. The CD-Extra is a multi-session CD. The first session contains audio data, which can be read by any CD player. The second session contains ROM data for the computer. Alongside audio data, the CD-Extra can also store video information, pictures or links to a homepage. The CD-Extra has replaced the mixed-mode CD. On this type of CD, the ROM data was put before the audio data. A few CD players did not recognise the ROM part and played the data, which could damage the HiFi.

CD-R (CD-Recordable)
This is a CD which can be recorded on only once. To do this you need a CD writer and either the software to go with it or a special 'Stand Alone' device. The standard is set out in the second part of the 'Orange Book'. The later pits of the CD are burned in with a laser beam.

These places are dull and they do not reflect back the laser light any more. This simulates the pits on a normal CD. Once you have recorded something on a CD-R, you can not record something else over it. It is possible, however, to store computer data on a CD-R in several sessions.

CD-R manufacturers have estimated that data will last up to ten or twenty years, but some firms have said up to fifty years.

CD-RW (Rewriteable)

The CD-RW is a further development of the CD-R that allows repeated recording on a disk. Just about every CD writer and CD player can write and read CD-RWs, too. The CD-RW is a bit more expensive than the CD-R and, according to the manufacturers, they can be recorded on up to 100 times.

▶▶ *The technical process of manufacturing a CD*

The glass master

The first stage of the CD manufacturing process is the glass mastering. The CD data on the pre-master (CD-R, U-Matic or DLT) are recorded on to a server and then transferred on to the glass master 1:1. The glass master used is a sheet of glass around 20 mm thick with a diameter of around 280 mm and coated with a photosensitive layer. The master data is picked out by a laser and burned into the photosensitive layer via a cache. The flow of data is four times as high as later, when the CD is being read by a CD player. When this process is finished, the glass master is heated up in a special kiln at around 310 degrees to protect the sensitive layer. As soon as the glass master is the same temperature as the oven, an aluminium alloy is evaporated on to the layer and the master is left to cool.

The sheet of glass is checked by camera for possible errors during the metal-coating process. Things which are checked include the even distribution of metal on the surface or possible errors in the material. The glass is then scanned once again by a laser. The laser checks that the data on the glass master is the same as the original.

The glass master can only be kept for around three to four days and therefore has to be processed further as quickly as possible. When quality control checks have been done, the glass master is ready to be electroplated.

Preparing the production masters

In the electroplating process the data on the glass master is copied on to non-sensitive disks, which are later used as a cutting pattern. The first stage involves copying a 'father' from the glass master. A nickel granulate is dissolved at around 80 degrees and the glass master placed in the nickel bath. The completely pure nickel covers the metal coating of the glass master. After about two minutes it is taken out of the bath and then takes around two hours to harden.

The completely pure coating of nickel is then separated from the metal layer of the glass master. The metal coating can also be removed from the master so that the sheet of glass can be cleaned and re-used.

The electroplating process is then repeated on the father. It is then coated with a mould release agent and once again dunked into the bath of nickel. This agent allows the father to be separated from the mother (a copy of the father). When the mother has dried out for around two hours, it is checked by laser for possible irregularities. When it has passed all these tests, the final production master (also called son or stamper) is produced.

There are two reasons why extra work is done to produce the stamper through a father and mother. An extra stage has to be introduced between the extremely sensitive glass master and the production of the stamper, as the glass master is too sensitive to produce a stamper directly from it. Another obvious reason is that at the end of the production process, all data has to be inverted on the stamper (which is negative), so that the information on the CD is the right way round (positive).

Production replication of the CDs

The stamper is mounted carefully inside a CD-stamping machine. Polycarbonate heated to a temperature of 340 degrees celsius is injected into the mould. A corresponding part with a flat surface presses the stamper into the liquid polycarbonate, giving it its final shape and helping to cool it down. A layer of industrial silver is evaporated on to the disk, which corresponds exactly to the CD's pits and lands. In the last stage of the manufacturing process, a protective coating is applied to the CD. Otherwise, the metal coating would get damaged through normal wear and tear or the ink on the label.

The finished CD is put on a spindle, ready to have the onbody label printed on it and to be packaged.

The final stage of putting the CD in a jewel case together with a booklet and inlay card is carried out by machine. Digipaks are boxed by hand by some manufacturers.

▶▶ *DVD – Digital Versatile Disc*

The DVD introduced in 1995, is a further development of the compact disc, and offers near infinite new possibilities.

With a storage capacity up to 25 times higher than that of a normal CD, plus a reading speed around 9 times as fast, the DVD offers new possibilities in all the areas it can be used. Music can be stored of a much higher quality on a DVD than on a CD. Videos can be made in different versions, including additional information (making of, background information about the actors and links to Internet sites).

How DVDs work
In contrast to CDs, the data on a DVD is stored in several layers. With CDs, what is called the substrate layer matches the thickness of the CD. When reading data, the laser penetrates almost the entire thickness of the CD, as the reflective silver coating is evaporated on to the top surface of the CD (directly underneath the label print). With a DVD, however, the substrate layer is only 0.6mm thick and two layers are stuck together. This makes it possible to record on both sides of the DVD. The layer on the top has a partially transparent layer of gold evaporated on to it.

As with a CD, the laser starts reading from the inside to the outside in a spiral track. If the laser reaches the edge of the top layer on the CD, it then focuses on the lower layer of the DVD and reads it from the outside, working inwards. The data from the top layer is 'superimposed' on to the bottom layer so quickly (in around 10 milliseconds) that there is no interference to the flow of data and the DVD can carry on uninterrupted.

Different types of DVD
There are four different storage capacities.

The DVD-5 (single-sided/single-layered) is the lowest storage capacity of all DVDs with 4.38Gb. Data is stored only on one side and on one layer of the DVD.

The DVD-10 (double-sided / single-layered) 8.75Gb is the same as the DVD-5, but recorded on both sides. In the future, DVD players will be equipped with 2 extra lasers which read DVDs on both sides, so they will not have to be turned over as at present.

The DVD-9 (single-sided / double-layered / 7.95Gb) is only recorded on one side, but uses both levels possible with a substrate coating. The storage capacity is smaller than that of a DVD-10, as the pits of the second (inner) level are 10% longer than those on the DVD5 or 10.

The largest storage capacity is offered by the DVD-18 (double-sided/ double-layered/15.9Gb). The DVD is recorded on both sides and uses both levels on each side. As it is extremely complex to produce the DVD-18, they are not currently mass-produced.

As with CDs, standards have been set for the various types of DVD. So far, standards have been established for the DVD-ROM, the Video-DVD and the DVD-Audio. There is, as yet, very little audio production on DVD due to the expense and the current low take-up of DVD-Audio players.

CHAPTER 11

►► Important information about record manufacture

If you are planning a 'special edition' on vinyl to go with your CD, or just want to bring out a single, there are many different things to watch out for. This chapter gives an insight into all aspects of record production.

You can find out about:

►► *Mastering records*
►► *Different types of vinyl format*
►► *Special formats*
►► *Different kinds of packaging*

▶▶ Mastering records

When you listen to a well-mastered LP from the vinyl era, you'll often notice the loud, dynamic songs come at the beginning of each side and quieter numbers or ballads come towards the end. The reason is not just to make the side fade out quietly. Unlike CDs, a record always spins at the same speed and , since the needle has to go further on the 'outer edge' than near the middle, there is room for the information required for dynamic songs. Quiet songs do not need so much.

This is something you should bear in mind when deciding on the order of your songs. Another thing you should do is distribute the songs evenly. The more songs there are on one side, the quieter the material will be, as the grooves are closer together.

Limit the extreme peaks of your songs. Cut out anything at the high end which is over 16-17 kHz. Do the same with everything under 20 Hz at the lower end of the bass scale, as anything in this range is not audible and makes lacquer cutting more difficult.

There are no other technical limitations which apply to vinyl mastering.

Lacquer cutting (Wax Cut) and Direct Metal Mastering
The master disc needed to make vinyl records is much the same as the glass master with CDs. There are two methods of manufacture, lacquer cutting and DMM (Direct Metal Mastering). The idea behind both procedures is to transfer the audio information to record format. The input material on CD or DAT is converted and cut into a master plate with a stylus.

Lacquer cutting
Lacquer (or acetate) cutting established itself in 1940 as the standard procedure for cutting records. A sapphire stylus cuts a groove into the lacquer at the right intervals. During the cutting process, the audio signal from the DAT or CD player is converted into a mechanical signal and transferred. The resulting 'master plate' is processed further in an electroplating procedure.

The master disk

A negative copy, called a father, is made from the electroplated master plate and has protruding ridges where the grooves were. The father is then recopied to make a positive master, known as the mother. A negative master is required, however, in order to make a record. That is why the mother is also recopied and the copy, the son (also referred to as a stamper), is used as a production master.

One stamper can be used to make around 1,000 records before wear and tear starts to affect the quality of the records. Another copy of the mother is made and used to produce a second son. This explains why the father is not used as a production master as a new father would require doing the very costly lacquer cutting again.

Direct Metal Mastering (DMM)

A groove is cut in the master record, but as with lacquer cutting, with a diamond-tipped stylus on a copper plate. This plate can be used directly as a mother to make a production mother cutting out two stages in the process. With lacquer cutting, repeated copying of the master has an effect on the quality of the finished records, but there is very little surface noise with DMM. Another advantage is that, with lacquer cutting, the record goes slightly out of shape after it has been cut into as the layer of lacquer curls back, or is slightly influenced by the adjacent groove. That does not happen when you cut into copper.

How do test pressings help?

After the production masters are made, test pressings are manufactured and sent to you by the manufacturers to check the quality of the records. The manufacturers only begin production on a large scale when you are satisfied with the test pressings, so listen to them very carefully.

The record-pressing process

The material used is mostly PVC (polyvinyl chloride) and vinyl acetate. Both of these materials are transparent and when soot is mixed in to make the surface of the record as smooth as possible, it gives vinyl its black colour. The viscous mass is poured into a pre-heated compression mould, the upper and lower moulds are pressed together and the record is kept inside the mould for a few seconds during the cooling process. At this point, a stylus trims off the excess vinyl.

After ten seconds the record has cooled down and is placed inside the cover. Alternatively, large orders are manufactured using an injection-moulding process.

▶▶ Different types of vinyl format

Different types of records can be distinguished by their rotation speed and diameter. The following standards established themselves as vinyl records developed from shellac records.

LPs (Long players)
The LP is a record format first brought out in 1949 by the Columbia record company. An LP has a diameter of 30cm (12 inches) and a rotation speed of 33⅓! rpm. If they are mastered through the lacquer cutting procedure, the recommended maximum playing time is between 24 and 27 minutes, according to the audio material. With those produced by DMM, the playing time can be around 10% longer, as the grooves can be cut closer together.

12-inch Singles
The 12-inch single was introduced in the 1970s to market remix and disco versions of successful songs. Like LPs, the maxi has a diameter of 30cm/ 12 inches, but a speed of 45 rpm (revolution per minute). The recommended playing time depends on the audio material but is usually eight to ten minutes per side (around 10% more with DMM).

Singles
Introduced in 1949 with the LP, the single owed its initial popularity to jukeboxes. They have a diameter of 17.5cm/7 inches and a rotation speed of 45 rpm. Around five minutes' material fits on each side (around 10% more with DMM).

EP (Extended play)
The EP corresponds to the single format, but has a different rotation speed of 33⅓! rpm. This gives a total playing time of up to nine minutes per side (around 10% more with DMM).

▶▶ Special formats

10-inch EP
The 10-inch or 25cm record is a rarer format. At 33⅓! rpm, the playing time is a maximum of 14-16 minutes. At 45 rpm the playing time is between nine and eleven minutes. It is as expensive to manufacture a 10-inch EP as a normal LP.

The 10-inch cover is more expensive to produce, as the machines to manufacture them are rare.

The Picture disc

Picture-discs consist of several layers, with a thin plastic disc in the middle covered with printed sheets of paper. Both sides of the record are glued on to this. With Picture disks, no soot is mixed in with the vinyl so the disk stays transparent, making the picture visible. Without the soot, the needle does not run as smoothly across the surface of the disc, and there is normally more surface noise than on black vinyl.

As well as round records, there are also special edition shaped discs cut into shape using laser cutting systems. To enhance the effect, shape discs are often also made as picture discs, with playing time depending on the shape.

Coloured vinyl

With coloured vinyl, a dye is mixed in with the vinyl instead of soot. Coloured vinyl records are a little bit more expensive to produce, as the dye must be mixed in individually. They do not sound quite as good as black vinyl, either.

Flexi (Sound foil)

The flexi is a very thin, flexible record in single format, recorded on one side only and often used to be enclosed with magazines. Nowadays, hardly any manufacturers make the flexi. The quality is very poor.

▶▶ Different kinds of packaging

Since the CD boom in the 1990s, record manufacture has decreased sharply. This has resulted in manufacturers and printers changing to CDs and CD packaging, so you have very few options if you are trying to package a record in an eye-catching way, and those you do have are very expensive.

To stay within reasonable financial limits when working on a vinyl record, you should stick to standard formats.

Label

Every vinyl record has to have a printed label in the middle, which is stuck on to the vinyl when the record is manufactured. Labels can be offset-printed in black/white or colour and they give details of the artist and the song, as well as information about the record company, the rotation speed, side (A or B) and the usual copyright information.

Inner sleeve

The vinyl record is put into a thin paper inner sleeve after it has been manufactured to protect it from dust and the rough inside of the cover. If you have anything printed on the inner sleeve, it will cost you as much as the cover. A cheaper alternative is the inlay sheet, which can be printed on one or both sides as required.

Disco sleeve

These are backless maxi covers made out of strong cardboard with a die-cut slot the size of an LP label which allows you to see the artist's name or the name of the song. Disco sleeves save you film output and printing costs.

Cover (or jacket)

The most common way to package a vinyl record is a cover (also known as a jacket). Durable cardboard is used, which is smooth and shiny on the outside and normal, untreated cardboard on the inside. Covers can be offset-printed (black/white or in colour) with a varnished finish as required. A matt finish, for example, makes the cover silky. As well as looking good, varnishing your cover will protect it from wear and tear, as well as stains. In addition, you can also have your cover embossed with silver or gold, have it printed using special (such as neon) colours or have it die-cut. That makes the LP look unique and increases its value. This will raise production costs, but Gatefold covers are suitable for double or triple LPs.

There are two types of cover for singles, the single and the EP cover, the only difference the thickness of the paper. The paper quality of single covers is 115gsm, EP covers 170gsm. Normal printing paper has a quality of 80gsm, which gives you some idea of what cover paper is like. Transparent PVC protective covers are also available to protect singles and LPs.

CHAPTER 12

▶▶Abbreviations and terminology

4-colour Printing:
The most common process for colour printing. By mixing the standard process colours Magenta, Cyan, Yellow and Key (black) most colours can be produced.

A&R:
Artists and repertoire. They search for new artists to sign to their label and are in charge of managing their careers.

Artist deal:
A recording contract stating that the company pays for all expenses, but also has a full say in what they do and do not do. (see: Record takeover agreement).

Booklet:
The book at the front of a CD containing photos, lyrics etc.

BPI:
British Phonographic Industry.

Break-even:
The point when all expenses have been covered and a profit is made.

CD-DA:
Compact Disc Digital Audio: CD with two channels and 44,100 16-bit samples per second.

CD-Text:
An extension of the Red Book standard. Besides information about the artist and the name of the title, the composer, conductor or style can be stored, too. Not all CD-writers, can write CD-Text however.

Commission:
On a commission basis, the goods are only paid for by the retailer when they are actually sold. The retailer also has the right to return unsold goods.

Compilation:
A CD featuring various bands or the hits of a single band.

Copyright:
Legal right to publish, broadcast, perform etc. a piece of music or writing. The right to the mechanical reproduction of music or other pieces of art.

Cover version:
Recording a song that has already been released by another artist/group.

DAT:
Digital Audio Tape.

Digipak:
Cardboard packaging with glued-in tray. Digipak is a registered trade mark, but other manufacturers of this kind of packaging call it D-Pac, Jade-Pac, etc.

Demo:
Short for a demonstration tape or CD recorded to send to a record company or promoter.

DVD:
Digital Versatile Disc. Similar to a CD, but with a DVD lasers can read two layers on one side with two different wavelengths. In addition, the length of the pits and lands have been reduced, leading to a greater storage capacity.

EAN:
European Article Number used for bar code generation.

Electroplating:
Technical process for creating production masters for vinyl records.

EP:
Extended Play vinyl single with a diameter of 7 inches and a rotation speed of $33\frac{1}{3}$ revolutions per minute.

Glass master:
The glass mastering comprises nearly the whole process of creating the production master. Data is transferred from the pre-master on to a server and then written by a laser on to a glass plate covered with a photosensitive layer (the glass master). The glass master is then coated with aluminium.

During the electroplating process a layer of nickel is created called a stamper (matrix). Finally, the stamper is mounted in to the injection moulding machine.

Image file:
The final data for a CD. After editing the CD with a piece of audio software, all the editing steps are taken into account when creating the image file.

Independent labels:
Small record companies whose main concern is music and not corporate bureaucracy.

Inlay card:
Printed card at the back of a CD jewel case with information on contents, bar code etc.

ISO9660:
Manufactured to ISO (International Organisation for Standardisation) 9660 is the most common file and directory naming standard, written in 1988. CDs to ISO9660 can be read by all operating systems.

ISRC:
International Standard Recording Code.

Jewel case:
Standard Transparent CD case.

Lacquer cutting:
Transferring the audio data on to lacquer from which the production master for the manufacture of vinyl records can be created.

Label:
Part of a record company. Big companies have various labels specialising in certain styles of music.

Label onbody print:
Details printed on to the CD.

LP:
(Vinyl-) Long play.

Mail order:
Retailing through the post.

Major label:
The big record companies: eg Sony Music, EMI, BMG, Warner, Polygram and Universal.

Mastering:
Editing the completely mixed master tape from the recording studio.

Maxi slimbox:
A jewel case CD, which is a bit thinner than the standard CD case.

Merchandise:
Products other than CDs related to an artist: such as T-shirts, mugs, posters, etc.

Mixdown:
Mixing of the recordings in a recording studio.

MCPS:
The organisation that collects and distributes 'mechanical' royalties to its composer and music publisher members that are generated from the recording of music.

Mechanical royalties:
The royalties earned from the recording of music (as against royalties from Broadcasting & Performance).

Offset printing:
Lithographic process for printing on to paper.

Paper label:
A round piece of paper in the middle of a vinyl record.

PDF:
Portable document format, software, now gaining widespread usage, for handling graphic files for printing. In some operations PDF can remove the necessity for lithographic printing film.

Pit/Land:
The CD's data is encoded as pits and lands (lower and higher areas).

PPD:
Published price to dealers, the average price which retailers pay the distributor.

POS:
Point of sale (retail).

PQ data:
Data stored in the CD's subcode containing information on the start and finishing times of the songs.

Pre-master:
CD-R generated according to the Red Book standard. From this CD-R the glass master is created by 1:1 copying at the manufacturers.

Record takeover agreement:
The record company receives the transfer-ready tape/CD from the artist. Thus the record company does not take a great financial risk, but does not a have a say in the artistic process either.

Red Book:
The technical specifications for CD-DA were laid out by Sony and Philips in their 1980 standard document, informally known as the Red Book.

Retail price:
The price of a CD in the shops.

RPM:
Revolutions per minute: the rotation speed of a vinyl record.

Silk-Screen Printing:
Standard printing process for CD onbody label.

Standard CD:
CD with a two-colour onbody label print and four-page booklet.

Standard production price:
The average manufacturing cost for a CD, used to work out the point at which costs are covered.

Start ID:
Starting point of a song on the CD.